England Needs a Revival

Jack Burton

England Needs a Revival

SCM PRESS LTD

0 334 02623 7

First published 1995 by
SCM Press Ltd
9–17 St Albans Place London N1 0NX

Typeset at The Spartan Press Ltd,
Lymington, Hampshire
Printed in Great Britain by
Biddles Ltd, Guildford and King's Lynn

To David and Thelma Bradford
Lord Mayor and Lady Mayoress of Norwich
1988–1989

whose civic leadership was
an inspiration to many in
the city, and beyond.

Acknowledgments

The extracts on pages 77–78 from D. H. Lawrence's essay 'A Propos of Lady Chatterley's Lover' (1930) and *Women in Love* (1930) are used by kind permission of the publishers, William Heinemann Ltd, Laurence Pollinger Ltd and the Estate of Frieda Lawrence Ravagli.

Contents

Preface

On the very day I was writing these words, two exciting things happened. In the morning, I received a St George's Day card from friends who believe firmly that England is a phenomenon worth commemorating and celebrating – as I do.

In the afternoon, I conducted a christening, a full-blooded, working-class, non-regular-churchgoing occasion, precisely the kind of christening more and more parsons seem hell-bent on avoiding. And I loved it, revelled in the immediacy and reality of it, and felt it was a valid, effective and worthy proclamation of the gospel.

In these two incidents, I saw the contents of this book illustrated graphically. England is a beautiful country, and its people have a goodly heritage. But England is sick, and the church doesn't understand why, or know what to do about it.

The simple truth is that England needs a revival. Nothing matters to it more than this. And we must all be ready to play our part, when the Spirit of God moves.

St George's Day 1995   Jack Burton

Colegate
Norwich

I

England, my England

The Christian church is flourishing in lands throughout the world. In many parts of Africa and China, the name of Jesus is being proclaimed, and the message of the gospel is being received with gladness. Here in England, it is good to be reminded frequently of these heartening facts. It sets our own unimpressive witness in context. When we become downcast at our failure to reach out effectively with the message of divine love; when the formula which would help us capture the hearts of this generation eludes us; and as we watch so much of our traditional work constricting – with congregations diminishing and little interest evident in the things of God – it is vital not to lose heart.

God isn't asleep, or grown old, or – worst of all – dead. God *is* in all times and in all places. 'In him we live and move and have our being.' And God is active – *doing* things – now. At this very moment, sharper than a two-edged sword, his word is piercing human resistance and ignorance and sin, bringing life and immortality to light through the gospel. At this moment, men and women are hearing about Christ, and committing themselves to the Way. And at this moment, the Holy Spirit is filling empty lives with energizing power, enabling weaklings to live victoriously and making dead bones live. It is happening now, and on an immense scale.

Let this knowledge thrill and enhearten us! Let it sink in, then be proclaimed, loud and clear! The movement to which we belong is not a clapped-out institution whose days are numbered. On the contrary, it is being true to its calling and pursuing its mission – and the harvest is great. God is not European – still less Anglo-Saxon! From moment to moment, his Spirit upholds this vast, unfathomable cosmos. On planet earth, our home, all lands and all people are precious to him. The church is growing. The word is being received eagerly and with great joy. That is the true picture – the overall context – in which our labours are set.

Nonetheless, such heartening knowledge remains only a partial consolation to those of us who love our native land, who believe its greatness is linked inextricably with its comprehensive Christian heritage, and who fear that those links are becoming ever more tenuous. The faith which helped shape everything, from our language to our landscape, is in danger of becoming a minority interest. There are still many who care: but dark and destructive forces are at work, too.

Today, many regard patriotism as an outmoded concept, a dirty word, a dangerous irrelevance for the residents of a global village. And if, in practice, patriotism means aggressiveness, contempt, and a spirit of haughty superiority, then it has, indeed, become the enemy of peace, the enemy of international understanding, and an enemy of the gospel. But, truly understood, patriotism is an expression of divine diversity and creativity. Different traditions, customs, insights, languages, and cultures are life-enhancing and enriching, and need not inevitably become pegs upon which to hang our hatreds, our aggressions, and our immaturities.

There is nothing wrong in cultivating an attitude of gratitude to those whose labours produced the society we have inherited. An awareness of history and a knowledge of our roots heighten the experience of living. They create and reinforce a sense of identity, a recognition of community, and a feeling of 'belonging', all of which are essential to the well-being of any society.

Of course, anything wholesome is capable of being perverted. Patriotism *can* become the last refuge of the scoundrel! When it becomes twisted, when it attempts to settle what it perceives to be old scores, and fights ancient battles all over again; when it looks with disdain upon the history and the dreams of other peoples, it deserves the contumely which it attracts. But the love for one's native land which is able to include a sense of sadness for the dark pages in its history is neither unworthy nor unChristian. I am warmed by the patriotism of those of other nationalities, and – by listening sympathetically and with interest – feel, somehow, able to share in it! Even, much closer to home, when the Scot (encouraged by his Tourist Board!) boasts of his whisky, tartan, haggis, bagpipes, porridge, lochs and heather, I warm to him. When he declares

> My heart's in the Highlands, my heart is not here;
> My heart's in the Highlands a-chasing the deer,

something leaps within me; I am there, too! True patriotism is mutually stimulating. It involves sharing the things we treasure, and discovering the treasures of others. Far from being a shameful thing, it is a celebration of diversity. We share one fragile earth. International and global obligations, to other countries and to the planet itself, should take precedence over all others. But God exists 'in the minute particularity of creation' – in the detail as well as the vastness. I know, as Nurse Edith Cavell so movingly reminded us, that 'patriotism is not enough'. But if I cannot love my country, which I have seen, how can I love a distant country, which I have not seen?

The other parts of the United Kingdom are dear to me, also; we hold much in common and belong together. But the ethos of Scotland, for example, differs from that of England. The opportunities and difficulties facing both church and nation differ, sometimes subtly, sometimes glaringly. I do not presume to address these differences. I speak of England. It sounds almost old-fashioned to do so, but there it is! In these terms I defend my sense of patriotism. England's story is my story, its shames and glories my own.

I am jealous for England's good name. I long for it to be known throughout the world for its compassion and integrity. I want the cross of Christ to be as central to those pages of its story, yet to be written, as it has been throughout the years of its long history.

The Christian message reached these shores whilst the same Roman empire, which had supervised the crucifixion, occupied and embraced this land. Successive invaders and settlers, with

varying degrees of sincerity and devotion, all accepted the
teaching of Christ. As a result, much that is good in the life and
history of this country, and many of the traditional attitudes
and features we take for granted, had their origin in the practice
of the Christian religion. Our schools and hospitals, our love of
liberty and our traditional sense of fair play – all can be linked to
the influence of the gospel. The parish churches which adorn
the landscape of England, together with the tiny wayside
chapels, symbolise a strand in our national identity of profound, incalculable, and unparalleled significance. In short, the
gospel of Christ has shaped the England we have inherited.

But what is happening now? Is the church, in England, still
generating the spiritual energy and moral power required to fire
the soul of the nation as it did, in a multitude of ways, in days
gone by? Forget, for the moment, the advances in Africa and
China. What is happening *here*? The harsh fact is that the
church is making an ever-diminishing impact on the lives of the
populace at large. Some denominations, parties, and sects are
attracting a growing following, but active participation in
'organized religion' is very much a minority interest. The gap
between the church and the majority of the people who live in
your street resists, resolutely, the most determined attempts to
bridge it.

I have dedicated the greater part of my life to pursuing the
ministry of a 'worker-priest'. This followed four years in
college, and five in the traditional circuit ministry of the
Methodist Church. I have tried to show the flag. I have
attempted to provide, by my presence, a reminder of the
existence of the church, and, on occasion, a demonstration of
caring ministry. But I have not persuaded hordes of people to
swarm across the divide (which I have tried to narrow) and into
the church.

Some people remain genuinely interested in what the church
says and does, though mostly, alas, as detached observers only.
They feel no involvement, and seek none. Sundays are spoken
for, and worship doesn't feature on their list of commitments.
Nor has its deletion occurred recently. The churchgoing habit
has been one of the myths of my lifetime. People have not

attended church in great numbers, other than in exceptional circumstances or on special occasions, for a very long time. Yet a recognition of the church persisted unchallenged: an intuitive awareness of its place in our history; an acceptance of its unique role in society; the acknowledgment, despite widespread failure to honour them, of Christian values.

In a profound and meaningful sense, England was a Christian country; and it is here, rather than in terms of church attendance, that the change has taken place.

Let me hasten to emphasize that this is not a comment on the multi-racial nature of England today. The presence within the social fabric of modern Britain of ethnic minorities who rejoice in their own languages, culture, history, religion and colour, is the source of an enrichment infinitely greater than all the misunderstandings, difficulties, and prejudices. Indeed, for the purposes of this present discussion the existence of a multi-racial society is an undoubted bonus, since many of those who have, this century, chosen to make this country their home retain a reverence for religion which we, whose forebears have lived here longer, have virtually jettisoned.

It is, of course, easy to dismiss sneeringly the phrase 'Christian country' when recalling the days, not long-distant, when children were sent up chimneys and down mines, a plethora of social evils flourished, and hypocrisy reigned, not least in the field of sexual attitudes. Yet, gradually, these issues were challenged and tackled. Christianity was not least among the sources of inspiration that provoked the vision of a new heaven and a new earth. If, among social reformers, there was a common language, many of its most ringing phrases came from the Bible. This Christianity went far beyond churchgoing. It was about culture. It may have fallen far short of the committed discipleship enjoined upon us by the New Testament, but at least it provided a moral chart and compass: some generally accepted points of reference.

I was born with the Second World War six weeks old, and my formative years, therefore, were those of the 1940s. The nation's links with its Christian heritage were still in place at that time – the respect for something which, if not personally and actively desired or pursued, was nonetheless valued and acknowledged. If Mother herself didn't go to church, she at least made a determined, if ultimately fruitless, effort to send me to Sunday School. The illogicality of it all was not lost, even upon a small boy. I counter-attacked in a variety of ways: protracted visits to the toilet became suddenly unavoidable as the hour for Sunday School drew near; other ruses were employed, and eventually my wishes prevailed. But the attempt, though vain, had been made; and even I understood that the church stood for something important. Times have changed. Times always change. But has the baby gone out with the bathwater?

The older one grows, the more difficult it becomes to make reliable judgments, or comparisons which are worth anything! It's an elementary fact of life that things are never what they used to be. And let's be honest – what a good thing that is! The benefits we enjoy as the result of modern technology are immense. Compared with earlier generations, we are richly blessed. In the days when I schemed to avoid Sunday School, I lived in a street of terraced houses where only one person owned a car. I still remember the number – it has nostalgic, almost mystical, overtones: CCL 943. Today, parked cars line both sides of that road, and buses no longer venture to manoeuvre between them. Some may feel I have not selected the happiest example to illustrate the benefits of progress, and on reflection, I would be inclined to agree. The private car has a great deal for which to answer. We have all bowed down and worshipped it, sacrificing our towns and villages to it, and threatening our environment with its emissions. Yet all of us, at sometime, have been grateful for a lift!

Beyond dispute, however, and plain for all to see, are the astounding advances in medical care which (human nature being what it is) we take now almost for granted. I would rather visit the dentist today than in the days of my childhood! So many good things adorn modern life – from the individual alarms in sheltered homes, to CDs – that it's unnecessary to compile a long list. All this Christians should be swift to acknowledge, not least because often they seem to be among the chief beneficiaries.

The benefits and advances in modern understanding extend beyond the scientific into the realms of the moral and spiritual, and we should be glad, not grudging, in our recognition of the fact. The images of terror and disaster which modern telecommunications thrust into our living-rooms provoke intense compassion and sadness, and a longing that things might be different. Many attitudes have changed for the better. Not very long ago, 'cowardice in the face of the enemy' led to a court-martial and a firing-squad. Today, no responsible person would attempt to maintain that ordinary human fear, let alone clinical shell-shock, constituted grounds for execution. For all our faults, we are immeasurably more merciful and more humane than we were only a few years back. To give young people the impression that they might as well pack up before they've even begun, because everything has gone to the dogs, and the best things have happened already, would be as wicked as it would be nonsensical. Incidentally, we have already instilled a disturbing sense of hopelessness among many of our young unemployed, which threatens both their own happiness and the stability of the community.

It is utterly vital to stress, and stress again, the good and positive aspects of modern living. Life is sweet, and can always be made even sweeter. I say these things, not to apologize in advance for the note I intend to sound in a moment, but because they are true. As we look at our country in the 1990s it isn't all doom and gloom that we see, thank heavens! Quite the opposite.

Yet, in a sense, that makes what I want to say next even more worrying.

2

The Dark Shadow

Bad things are happening in England: very bad, and deeply disturbing. We hear of them, we sense them, we experience them: and we don't know what to make of them. This is where getting old complicates matters. When I was a young man, I didn't hesitate to make judgments! Whether or not I was in possession of the full facts, I had an opinion on every subject under the sun, and was seldom slow to express it. It dawned on me only slowly that most of my views were based upon ignorance, prejudice, and a pitiable inexperience. I didn't stop pontificating, but I believe I became more cautious! Caution becomes cowardice, however, if it prevents us speaking out when we know we ought.

The fact is, of course, that bad things have always happened: very bad, and very frequently. As an enthusiastic local historian, I have perused old, faded newspapers for hour after hour. I know, from these studies, that violent, criminal, uncaring, and anti-social attitudes are not new. For me, the difficulties arise when I attempt to quantify and evaluate. Is there more . . . ? Is it worse . . . ? Responsible and accurate judgments are not necessarily made easier by the fact that we see and hear more news and comment on current affairs than any generation before us. The fact that we know particular things are happening certainly doesn't mean that nothing like it ever happened before. The chances are, it did! The making of comparisons and relative judgments in matters of morality, religion, and politics is a combined minefield and nightmare, unless your viewpoint is simplistic or biased. If you believe in something akin to the inevitability of progress – a touching faith – or if you truly believe that England has sold herself to the

Devil, the issues are, I suppose, more clear-cut. But if neither of those attitudes appeal to you as being sustainable or realistic, a measure of evaluation becomes necessary, and the effort and the risk involved in making judgments unavoidable.

Having prepared the ground as carefully as possible, I have to climb off the fence. I do so with some reluctance, and no little embarrassment, but also with a sense of relief that my fears are, at last, out in the open. When every precaution has been taken against prejudice (and vested interest!), I cannot, personally, avoid the conclusion that something threatening, sinister, and vicious is eating at the very soul of the nation. I don't like saying it, and I hope I'm wrong. I long to be persuaded that those words are irresponsible, foolish, and meaningless. Certainly, they are not my usual style! What, then, has provoked me, and what evidence have I? Nothing that would stand up in a court of law, that's for sure! But that's nothing new! Facts and interpretation always go hand-in-hand, and I have an habitual tendency to rely heavily on gut feelings and intuition, occasionally laying myself open to the charge of making allegations I am unable to substantiate.

This time however, I would defend myself warmly against any such charge. I have no axe to grind. I am not clinically depressed over church attendance statistics. My theology sees God active throughout human society, and not confined to ecclesiastical structures. I rejoice at the fruits of education, and marvel at the discoveries of science. If the maturity of modern man causes him to cast aside religious categories as unnecessary intellectual and social baggage, I may beg to differ but am not heartbroken. God has more ways than one of achieving his ends. My unease is the unease of a broad-minded, catholic-spirited, somewhat worldly Englishman, who despises the hypocrisy inherent in Christianity (particularly in the realms of wealth and sex), and who is glad to see such attitudes exposed and rejected. It is also the unease of one who cares deeply for his country, and wonders what is happening to it; and who loves the church, and simply wonders...

Although I conceded that, often I allow myself to be guided

by the emotions as well as the intellect, and that some of my attitudes are the product more of instinct than of carefully researched studies, I believe that certain, significant changes in social behaviour and political trends can be demonstrated more-or-less objectively. My examples, alas, are not startlingly original. Indeed, they are simple in the extreme. To me, however, they are no less instructive for that.

Crowd control costs my favourite football team thousands of pounds each season. Large numbers of police and stewards are needed to segregate rival supporters, and minimize the threat of violent disorder. I know from personal experience that it wasn't always like that. Obviously, wherever large crowds assemble – and they used to be larger than today – police supervision is necessary, and a few arrests inevitable. But when I first began watching football matches, we used to be *pleased* if some visiting supporters stood near us, bedecked conspicuously in their team's colours. In unfamiliar accents they would tell us about their game the previous week, talk about the early start they'd made that morning to their journey, and give a confident prediction of the day's result. There would be a little banter, some good-natured leg-pulling, and plenty of laughter. The good play of each team would be sportingly (if grudgingly!) acknowledged and applauded. The notion of chanting obscenities, spitting, smashing shop windows, or killing each other simply didn't arise.

If anyone imagines I have drawn a cloth-capped caricature of a post-war golden age which never existed, they are mistaken. Anyone over fifty will recognize my thumb-nail sketch. How innocent we must have been, some may think; how naive! No! We were behaving in a natural, normal, civilized, unexceptional, English, Christian manner. This, at least, is not an illusion induced by advancing years. The change is obvious, breath-taking, and profoundly depressing. So, too, is the staggering increase in lawlessness, at all levels, which has exploded in our face over the recent years. Crime figures were causing concern thirty years ago, but they were as nothing compared with what is happening now. Statistics are almost irrelevant. I no more doubt the reality of the immense growth in anti-social behaviour which has occurred comparatively recently than I question my own sanity.

I have lived for over a quarter of a century at the heart of an attractive English provincial city. I have not been surrounded by the urban wastelands of the great metropolitan areas, but by ancient streets and historic buildings. My inner-city experience has been lively and noisy, but genteel in the extreme when compared with that of those who have endured genuine inner-city privation. Nonetheless, it has convinced me that attitudes of lawlessness have reached proportions which merit serious concern. In the immediate vicinity of my church and home, we have experienced a range and degree of criminal activity unimaginable not long ago. From relatively trivial matters like the theft of milk from doorsteps, and the aggressive and reckless riding of cycles on the footpath (which, incidentally, is not trivial if you happen to be frail), the sad catalogue passes through theft from cars (on an almost routine basis), theft of cars, and theft of cycles, onward and upward to serious unprovoked assaults (sometimes in daylight), and murder/manslaughter. Twice my own home has been burgled, twice within a few months I was awakened to find the street beneath my window filled with fire engines attending arson attacks. Of these one was on my church (which came within an ace of being destroyed), and the other involved a property adjoining my home, thus endangering my entire family.

This quiet city, a hundred miles east of anywhere, now enjoys its regular share of armed robberies. Those of us who have known it for many years frequently stare at the *Evening News* with incredulity. That such things should happen *here*! It is small beer, of course, compared with what many others are having to endure. We are still catching up. My point is that – without question – an enormous change has taken place. And it is not a change for better.

In the early 1960s I spent two years in a tough area of Glasgow (a city I grew swiftly to love). It was not long after the mass murderer Peter Manuel had horrified the entire country. I walked the streets of that city, entered the closes of decaying tenement blocks, crossed muddy yards in the darkness of

winter, and have no recollection of feeling uneasy or
threatened. How different it can feel in provincial England,
today! Part of that difference, no doubt, is middle age, with all
the limitations (and experience!) it brings. But part is also the
knowledge that changes have taken place – hateful and
grotesque changes – which have made our streets less safe than
we formerly assumed.

If this is silly, irresponsible, and alarmist talk, I apologize
with all my heart. But my failing, I suspect, is one of
understatement. Anyone who has recently had dealings with
the police will have realized quickly that they are close to being
utterly swamped by the sheer volume of their work-load. The
law-breakers, meanwhile, have acquired a new confidence, and
possess little fear of the law. I think back to the gang of
youngsters I knew very well a generation ago, which included
one or two minor law-breakers, and again I sense the change.
Everything has moved up a gear. The lawlessness is fiercer,
more determined, more ruthless.

On the roads, too, there is important evidence of change –
although, once more, it is difficult to evaluate, to prove, to be
sure. I've driven buses for twenty-eight years, and my impression is that perceived wrongs – real or imaginary – are much
more likely than heretofore to provoke the furious response of a
thrusting, upright finger. When such gestures emanate from a
car containing children among its passengers, one can only
imagine the accompanying 'verbals', and shudder with despair
at the impact being made on the impressionable minds of the
generation to come.

Amid all that is wholesome and good about this present age,
there are changes and social trends we ought to monitor
carefully, to ensure they are not undermining the progress so
evident in other fields. Sociologists, politicians, historians,
criminologists and theologians must bring the light of their
respective disciplines to bear upon the England we see before us
in the last years of this millenium – to scrutinize, measure,
encourage, and warn. And, if I may say so, they want to get a
move on! For, however partially and incompletely, the man or
woman in the street senses plainly that something is not right.

This conviction is reinforced by watching the pathetic stream of human flotsam and jetsam to be found on our streets, in numbers which seem not to be decreasing. There are unemployed young people, with time on their hands. There are large numbers of homeless. There is more begging than most of us can ever recall, sometimes intimidatory in manner. There are people – again, usually young – standing in doorways and at street corners, watching and waiting. Some are simply killing time; but others are looking for opportunities; making sure the coast is clear. (This is a dispassionate observation – ask any milkman, policeman, or city-centre resident. There is an indefinable quality about bearing and body-language, which usually separates the person taking the air from someone potentially up to no good.) Most sad are the poor men and women with obvious special needs who often appear to require greater support than we, as a community, seem willing, now, to give them. They roam the streets in all weathers, not easy to help, yet somehow a challenge and a rebuke. No one with an ounce of humanity wants such people locked away. 'Care in the community' is an enlightened slogan. Without realistic funding, however, it can become a cruel, hollow, and empty phrase.

There has always been unemployment, homelessness, and mental illness; thieves, beggars and eccentrics (of all types, including clergymen!) are facts of life. But the incidence of these phenomena, and the acuteness of the problems associated with them, are linked inevitably to the prevailing political philosophies. This is not the place to score party political points. Nevertheless, the fact remains that policies which have been advocated openly and pursued single-mindedly for a decade-and-a-half have to be judged in the light of their social consequences. Some of the disquieting changes in the fabric of England today are the result not of social developments of a random nature, but of deliberate political decisions. I'm not saying, 'It's all the government's fault'; but I am saying that the Tories are particularly involved, because their policies were strikingly successful, and helped to fashion what we have become. So there it is! Am I becoming increasingly confused? Is all this a middle-aged man's paranoia, or is it a bewildered realist's sober assessment of the changes affecting England today? You must decide! One journalist averred recently that 'the English are astonishingly rude, blazingly ignorant, professionals at illiberalism, consumed by the meanest politics'. By contrast, I have nearly over-balanced trying to avoid wild expressions and sweeping judgments. I have aimed to accentuate the positive, and to celebrate the things which are good and right. Even at this moment I am being afflicted with a bad attack of cold feet, lest I be branded politically, sociologically, or theologically incorrect! I want to withdraw most of what I have said. But I cannot. Something is seriously wrong which it will take more than changes of government to put right, and every thoughtful person knows it, and wonders – with apprehension and a sense of foreboding – where it will all lead.

If I had to summon one image to symbolise that foreboding and unease, it would be the chilling video picture of the small child being led away from the supermarket to a cruel death, his tiny hand held trustingly in that of an older child. This archetypal big-brother image was supplemented and reinforced by the child of similar age, visible in the background of the picture, with a hand held securely by its mother. The contrasting fates of the two children gave the picture a truly chilling quality, which filled me with horror the instant I saw it, long before the appalling details of the case became known. Great crusades cannot be launched on single incidents, however sensational; but this tragedy provoked a stab of self-awareness and self-doubt to flicker across the collective consciousness of the nation, as well it might. A child murdered by other children. It's not unknown: yet if that case didn't cause the most hardened or complacent among us to ask, 'what kind of society are we creating?' then nothing will. And if the cruel tortures inflicted upon the Manchester girl, Suzanne Capper, and the unspeakable manner of her murder at the hands of other young people didn't affect us in the same way, we really are in trouble.

No, no – a sickness afflicts us. Its grosser manifestations afflict only a minority, thank God; yet I suspect we are all tainted. Our lives are inter-linked; we are members one of another.

3

Springs of Darkness

What has brought about this state of affairs? If only we were looking for one simple answer! I write neither as sociologist nor psychiatrist. I make no pretence of being other than someone who merely reads the papers, goes to church, and loves his country. But even to the likes of me certain factors seem significant. I need mention them only briefly, since none of my observations are startlingly original.

Unhesitatingly, at the top of the list I place the fact that, for the past half-century, we have lived under the shadow of the bomb. The past two generations have grown up with weapons of mass destruction part of everyday language: two generations which have had to adjust to the monstrous knowledge that we possess the technical ability to end everything, and destroy the entire planet. It is impossible to exaggerate the emotional and psychological impact this awareness has had upon the youth of the nation. Nobody could escape being affected. How common it was – and still is – to hear a young person say, resignedly: 'It doesn't matter, because we're probably going to blow ourselves up, anyway.' Such unparalleled anxieties, such an unprecedented burden, could do no other than create a well of unfathomable, negative emotion. When the ultimate nightmare – a scenario formerly the harmless preserve of cranks and religious devotees – became a matter-of-fact scientific reality, most people found it difficult to cope. We may have concealed our horror, but the shock was deep, and the damage lasting. No preparation could ever have been adequate to receive knowledge of this nature; and, perhaps worst of all, our spiritual reserves, as a nation, were at a low ebb. The signs were not good; and, predictably, the result has been bitter.

Young men and women, before whom the future should have stretched invitingly and endlessly, suddenly realized that there might not be a future at all. Life's cruel, ever-present element of hazard they could accept. In a perverse way, it almost added spice to life. A friend's death on a motor bike . . . a suicide . . . these were terrible shocks: they were unnatural, but in a natural kind of way! This was different. The frailty of human existence was uncovered and exposed with an unfeeling, unsparing starkness which itself posed a threat to that very frailness. Our emotional and mental capabilities were stretched to their limits and beyond. And the toothpaste could never be squeezed back into the tube. This knowledge was immutable. Humankind would have to live with it for ever, poised eternally on the edge of a volcano of destruction.

It is becoming hard to rekindle the impact made by that awareness when first it began to sink in. When the chips were down, few people entertained over-optimistic opinions of the human race en masse. Our track record was not encouraging. Someone, somewhere, at sometime – wilfully or unwittingly – would unleash the unspeakable. The odds seemed stacked heavily against rationality and survival. Thus the children of the twentieth century lost any lingering innocence. A grain of hopelessness was planted in every young heart, and the grain grew quickly to produce a blighted harvest. Its characteristics became all too familiar. Insecurity, resentment, fear, a propensity to live for the moment and to grab 'what you can, when you can' – all these were common reactions to our nuclear knowledge. Saddest of all was the bravado which attempted to hide the frustration, the desperation, the bitter sense of injustice, the unshed tears at a wrong that could never be righted.

Fears unchecked can become self-fulfilling, engendering attitudes which make more possible that which is dreaded. And nations are affected, as well as children! Lift the insecurity, resentment, the willingness to grab, and the bravado, to an international level, and the dangers are obvious. The nuclear threat is here to stay. As individuals we appear to have begun to come to terms with the fact, to accommodate it as best we can, to relegate it from the forefront of our conscious minds. Nobody can mourn for ever. But the damage has been done and, in truth, will continue to be done until a new type of world government makes the threat of a nuclear holocaust utterly unimaginable. That age has not yet dawned.

It is, therefore, neither fanciful nor alarmist to see in the shadow which falls across England a chilling reminder of the shadow of nuclear night. The bomb has affected profoundly the way we think and act and feel. People who are not sure they will have a tomorrow will not worry unduly about the consequences of their behaviour today.

Second on my list of significant contributory factors I place the impact of television, and what might be termed the 'video culture'. When St Paul wrote to the Philippians, he gave them sound psychological advice which can have been seldom more beautifully expressed: 'Finally, brethren, whatsoever things are true, whatsoever things are honest, whatsoever things are just, whatsoever things are pure, whatsoever things are lovely, whatsoever things are of good report; if there be any virtue, and if there be any praise, think on these things.' The lesson is clear. If you eat bad food, you will contaminate your body and become ill. And if you fill your mind with trivial and unworthy rubbish, you risk becoming a trivial and unworthy person. There's no great mystery about it.

Recently, a group of leading child psychologists admitted that they had naively underestimated the strong links between violent videos and crime. While recognizing that experts must have reliable data to hand before rushing to make sweeping judgments, one could still only marvel at the lateness of their verdict. Their naivety was of the kind that gives experts a bad name.

I was first attracted to my wife because she was pretty and kind, but the fact that her parents had a television probably clinched it! What was, to me, less than forty years ago a novelty has become an elementary part of everyday life, assimilated and taken for granted in the way that now we take every new discovery swiftly in our stride. Our wonder soon fades, a fact to which I shall return.

To affirm that modern electronics – television, computers, videos – has revolutionized our lives is to understate the obvious. Visual impact is second to none in its power to influence our opinions, and affect our behaviour. Television is a potent medium – and it is good! To the elderly and house-bound, it is a boon beyond compare; and to us all, it constitutes a rich source of education and entertainment.

But, like most things, it has a dark side, with immense potential to cause harm. News and programmes of current affairs are appreciated by everyone, and we demand accuracy and detail. Occasionally, however, I wonder what effect upon us the images of war and deprivation have, which we absorb in a constant stream. I am musing aloud, and not making judg-ments – nobody watches the news more avidly than I. But how much violence, death, and suffering can we assimilate safely? Copious draughts, perhaps. Yet there is a two-fold danger.

First, it has a profoundly depressing effect upon sensitive people, which is magnified greatly by their inability to respond in a meaningful and practical manner. The knowing, plus the inaction, generate a kind of guilt; and guilt, untreated, is always unhealthy. The amount of 'bad news' we can absorb safely before our own peace of mind is overtaken by dark and negative emotions is a very pertinent issue. It sounds selfish to set out the situation so coldly and starkly, but it has to be faced. It takes most people all the resources they can muster to deal with the anxieties and crises which directly touch their own lives. The majority, however, are still capable of offering much more, empathizing with a wide circle of neighbours and friends, and offering support and help in times of need. But we are the first generation to be exposed visually to a daily diet of detailed suffering from the four corners of the earth, and it is weighing people down, and putting into their hearts a sadness, a heaviness, and feeling of helplessness.

The second danger is probably even more alarming. Our sensibilities become blunted. To protect ourselves, we sub-consciously create an emotional equivalent to the ozone layer in an attempt to minimize the impact of harmful impressions. We eat large meals as we blink at pictures of emaciated children, or bodies broken in war. A hardening takes place, a steeling of the spirit. And a certain blurring of the lines occurs, between fantasy and reality and between what is acceptable and what is abhorrent. We grow accustomed to seeing so many images of violence that it becomes increasingly difficult truly to shock us.

These are some of the risks involved; not in watching bizarre programmes, or pseudo-pornography, nor any of the more obviously-questionable material, but in watching something as sensible and important as the news. So intense and immediate is the impact of the visual! It would be silly, dishonest and cynical to assert that from this point onward, it is downhill all the way! So much which is good is on offer, and our personal preferences vary widely. What is, to me, of no consequence, might be meat and drink to you! Suffice to say, however, that some televised material inevitably provokes the question: 'What impression is this making on receptive and uncritical minds?'

The new video market means that access to vivid visual images is now easier and wider than ever. Inevitably, this material is not subject to the same regulation and restraints as broadcast television. Videos, of any type, can be shown at any time, and to any audience. Horror movies, pornographic films, and material purporting to dabble in the occult are all easily obtainable. They have become, for those who seek them, an unexceptional feature of our modern way of life. Nobody can prove the precise impact they have on the minds of those who watch them: but it can hardly be other than a coarsening, a cheapening, and a dangerous blurring of perceptions.

The scope for conveying visual images is ever widening and, with it, the opportunities for the unscrupulous to profit from the dissemination of darkness. A recent police investigation in Norfolk confirmed the existence of a network of pornographic material to which access could be gained simply by tapping in to any ordinary computer in the viewer's home. What a distance we've travelled from the days of dirty postcards. Our technology – in this, as in every field – has outstripped our morality; our scientific abilities dwarf our spiritual resources. We have not coped well with the overwhelming impact of modern electronics and telecommunications in the second half of this

century. That which repeatedly enters the eye will eventually
be found written upon the heart. Spiritually under-nourished,
we have gorged ourselves on visual wonders, and failed to
recognize and distinguish between wholesome nourishment
and deadly poison.

Everything I know about drugs could be written on the
back of a postage stamp. Fortunately, others have studied the
subject more closely. They are unlikely to disagree when I list
the moden fascination with drugs as my third grave cause for
concern. It mystifies me, beyond words, why young men and
women should want to inject alien substances into strong,
healthy bodies, or be prepared to risk swallowing a handful of
dubious tablets. To me, both practices fly in the face of every
natural instinct for self-preservation. Even the empty hopelessness of inter-city poverty would not push me down that road
– or so I imagine.

Such customs were unknown in my youth. I was never
offered anything more noxious than a sherbet lemon. Again
how times have changed! The new interest in drugs was part
of the reaction to the nuclear threat, and 'living for kicks'
became a popular philosophy among young people. If everything could end at any time, it made sense to live for the
moment: to seek every experience which might provide
insight, and to pursue every sensation of pleasure, without
thought of the consequences. Now we have an international,
multi-million-dollar industry, promoting and servicing a
sub-culture of evil.

One assumes there must be people quietly getting on with
their drug-taking, in private, who are receiving immense
fulfilment, and are on the verge of sharing their precious
insights with the rest of the human race. I, for one, look
forward to hearing from them. There are, manifestly,
thousands more who don't seem to be getting anything very
special from their addiction, nothing, certainly, which has
ever engendered in me the faintest suspicion of envy. Hollow-
eyed, gaunt, sallow-looking, sick with worrying where the
next money is coming from to satisfy their craving, they look
unlikely sources of insight and enlightenment. On the con-

trary, they look pathetic and, not infrequently, dangerous. They are poor advertisements for their habit.

We live in days when, far from immediately challenging wrong-doers, it is prudent to be careful how you so much as look at them. If they happen to have taken drugs recently, their enhanced perception might reveal to them that they ought to kill you. Vicious and unprovoked attacks are no longer rare. Sometimes, in expressing regret, defending solicitors have the gall to refer to their clients' drug-taking in words which suggest not merely an explanation but an excuse. When, in addition, we are told the extent of the drug problem in prisons, and how impossible it is to stamp out, the whole thing assumes nightmarish, Alice-in-Wonderland proportions. The shadow which falls across England is, in part, chemically induced.

It all points to a profound spiritual emptiness, and too many people have been persuaded to assuage their hunger in the wrong way. Human life is complex and mysterious, and there is a longing in the hearts of all men and women for meaning, insight, and illumination. Assuredly, 'Man shall not live by bread alone'. And there is no need for him to do so. The pathways to that enlightenment for which our spirits cry out are numerous: music, meditation, art, literature, religion, comtemplation, poetry, nature. Along those paths new discoveries are made, fresh possibilities present themselves, dimensions of life and experience hitherto unimagined beckon, and invite exploration. All are capable of disturbing and challenging – but all are life-enhancing and health-giving, in contrast to the way of drug addiction, which threatens health and impairs personality.

All pathways to perception – including drugs – help us to reach beneath and beyond the surface to other, deeper layers of reality. But there are risks. We can only endure these higher truths in small doses. Just as the ozone layer protects us from being harmed by the life-giving rays of the sun, so our finite human minds seem to be protected from the over-powering immediacy of – of what? Reason fails; our words falter and expire. From God! That has to be the answer. From the unimaginable, frightening, all-consuming glory of a God defined as the Reality-which-lies-behind-all-things. Here, surely, is the ultimate paradox, the ultimate human dilemma. We cannot cope with too much knowledge: despite our achievements, we are puny, transient creatures, apparently lacking the apparatus to 'bear very much reality'. Yet we have an insatiable hunger, curiosity, and longing – for greater knowledge, for a sense of meaning, identity and purpose, for feelings of reassurance and acceptance, for experiences of unity and harmony with all that is, seen and unseen. In traditional religious terms, we have a hunger for God. Tension therefore, even danger, is inherent in what it means to be a human being, existing only within the conditions imposed by this paradox: restricted in body and mind, yet fired by a free, restless, endlessly-inquiring spirit.

This 'other knowledge' which we seek – those 'revelations', those treasured moments – we seem able to assimilate only in relatively small doses, from time to time, perhaps growing as we go. A symphony, or a song; a silence, or a scent, a friendship or a film; daybreak or evensong; a solemn mass or an orgasm – all effect changes in us and in our perceptions. And it is no coincidence that all these precious things can make you cry (or feel like crying) just as easily as they can exalt your spirit – and do so frequently. At such moments, the illumination and insight is pushing back our mind's protective barrier, increasing our awareness, making us 'larger', 'richer' people – but also more vulnerable, and more exposed.

All human beings are called to undertake this journey. But drug-taking is a short cut. It demands the sensations without the effort, save that of acquiring the wherewithal to obtain the drugs (when every trace of scruple or conscience is obliterated utterly). But the discipline of seeking is also our defence. Those who toy with drugs, even as an escape from lives empty and without hope, are risking health, sanity and peace of mind. They are tampering with forces which, once unleashed, may well destroy them. I am not talking here about a pint of beer, a glass of wine, or a cigarette. And I am certainly not talking about the use of prescribed drugs for medical purposes. I am talking about the drug culture which has emerged and flourished over the past thirty years. It is a curse upon our land.

As fourth on my sombre list of the springs of darkness I simply note the ever-accelerating rate of change which has characterized life in England since the war. It has contributed hugely to the creation of a sense of insecurity and a crisis of identity which, to a greater or lesser degree, seems to afflict us all. Streets, customs, institutions, many of which had endured for centuries, have been swept aside on a surging tide of unprecedented change which has left the world almost unrecognizable to anyone over fifty who dares to look back and remember. The process is continuing, with an almost bewildering rapidity. Before I could acquire a good record player, everyone else had moved on to compact discs!

Roots are important. And a sense of history is vital – not the learning of dates, but an awareness: of our place in the scheme of things; of the continuity of communities; of our relationship to other people – past and present – as the source of our own identity. Change is not evil. Often, it is good, and we should strive to see the hand of God in it. But rapid social change is hard to assimilate as, one after another, customary and traditional points of reference vanish before our eyes. It is unsettling, and leaves us unsure of ourselves, lacking in confidence and suspicious. We don't know who are our friends and who our enemies. We don't know which changes to welcome, and which to deplore.

Again, it is our scientific skills which are largely responsible. In the 1950s the private car began to achieve ascendency over public transport and television tempted people to stop going out to do things for themselves and just watch other people. These two changes alone produced incalculable social consequences, but they were followed immediately by a never-ending stream of new wonders, fresh discoveries, and endless changes to all things both great and small. Today, we have transplants and by-passes, motorways and by-passes, supermarkets, micro-chips, take-aways and AIDS. Wherever we look – from village life to the realms of industry and commerce – the picture is the same: development, progress, and change and all on a scale and at a break-neck pace hitherto unknown.

This all-embracing process, this new great fact of life, has had not only a destabilizing, but also a dehumanizing effect. Nothing seems fixed or dependable any more, nothing permanent. The signposts have gone, and we are left feeling like little lost children. The best that many of us can do is to hang on by our finger-tips, pretend we're enjoying it, and make up a few new rules as we go along! But it isn't always easy. St Paul's reminder that 'here we have no abiding city' has been brought home to no generation more forcefully than our own. In England today, where science reigns, customs, traditions, values, and standards are all in the melting-pot. It's difficult to be sure about anything: hard to know where we are, and who we are, and what it's all about. We've been overwhelmed, and cut down to size, by our own cleverness. Tomorrow will bring some new wonder, some new changes, some more alterations, some more anxieties. Young people may handle the pace of modern living better than the old, but they are not escaping unscathed. The shadow across our land falls on a people confused and bewildered, and longing for some solid ground on which to stand.

The political attitudes which have prevailed in recent years have contributed significantly to our national malaise, and I place them fifth on my dark list. One writes with hesitancy and a proper caution. This is emphatically not a political pamphlet. Nonetheless, it is a simple matter of historical record that one set of political ideas has dominated the life of this country through four parliaments, having been endorsed repeatedly at successive general elections. The actions of a government which has been so long in power cannot avoid scrutiny in any review of contemporary Britain, even in what is, essentially, a religious study. Attempts to assess philosophies and policies are inevitably contentious, since we all have our own political opinions and prejudices. Speaking personally, though, and with bluntness, I am appalled at the change in social attitudes which has taken place in recent years. The hearts of many have become hardened, and a spirit of selfishness has overtaken us.

The remarkable achievements of 'the Thatcher years' should never be underestimated. Problems which had been side-stepped for many years were tackled head on, sometimes with courage and imagination. Entrenched attitudes, damaging the nation, were changed. These things could not be achieved painlessly – and they certainly were not! Thatcherism altered, fundamentally, the thinking of the nation. But in which direction? In my view, away from the notion of society as a community of people who know they belong together, and acknowledge responsibility for one another, towards an attitude which sees individuals, first, as rivals and competitors, and which risks contempt for those who are not 'achievers'. The infamous phrase, 'There is no such thing as society,' summarizes the attitude neatly. This poison spread rapidly, feeding on the baser instincts of the electorate with devastating effect. Many very rich people became very much richer; many poor people became still poorer. One witty cartoonist depicted a toff, holding a collecting tin, with a placard hung around his neck which read 'Not rich enough', while a down-and-out, begging under the railway-arch, tossed a coin into the tin . . . It was a perceptive and pointed comment. The greed of the rich, in recent years, has been brazen; and they have enjoyed collusion and every encouragement in their sinfulness.

With unemployment running high, mean-spirited acts like the substitution of loans for grants, and the curtailment of benefits, served only to increase pressure upon the most vulnerable. Not all poor people commit crime, thank heavens! But there are obvious connections between poverty and those crime figures we profess to deplore, and not least in the number of drug-related offences. When an unpopular government, whose philosophy and policies have contributed to social instability and increases in crime, adopts a high profile on issues of law-and-order in desperate attempts to regain electoral support, hypocrisy and cynicism plumb new depths. Greed, however, has so soured the national spirit and impaired our insight and judgment that this is precisely the kind of sleight-of-hand likely to succeed. My contempt for contemporary Tory attitudes cannot be concealed, and I no longer bother to try. If a shadow falls across England today, the politicians have a lot to answer for. And – it must be emphasized – not Tory politicians alone.

The sixth item on my list of negative influences blighting our common life is the obvious complaint you would expect from a parson: the rejection of religion. A great swathe of the population has abandoned all interest in religious thought or practice. They have left England with a legacy of high ideals and noble principles which are dry and brittle because they are not constantly being renewed, and no longer form part of a living tradition. We have, of course, for far too long lived on our religious capital, and have ploughed little back into the nation's spiritual treasury.

The reasons for this rejection have been sought and analysed, ad nauseum. In a sense they are now academic, for the rejection has been overwhelming. Three factors have been particularly significant, and I mention them merely in passing. Science is perceived as having 'disproved' religion; the unutterable horrors of the First World War inflicted permanent damage not only upon an entire generation but upon the very soul of the nation; and – despite a pageant of noble exceptions – the church has been construed as the handmaid of the rich and privileged.

So we have a people with no religion – and not making out very well, despite putting on a brave front. They have sport and the arts; they have pop-music, cars, expensive holidays and electronic gadgetry – and, at the heart of it all, a great void. Religion, in some form or another, is always in the air. The nature of human beings means it cannot be kept off the agenda for long. But in England, today, it meets no informed response from people fast becoming religious illiterates. Their threadbare spiritual garments are painfully obvious. They are bemused by the fundamentalist sects reaching towards us, often from America, and are pathetically ill-equipped to counter the insidious influences that radiate from them. Their national identity has been broadened by immigration – including many who belong to other religions – but what should have been (and frequently has been) a source of enrichment has become, for some, a source of insecurity and confusion. Above all, they are under siege from the threatening and destructive influences to which I have referred: nuclear knowledge, the video and drug cultures, continual and rapid change, and repressive political policies. To deal with these challenges, they are woefully ill-equipped. They have few religious reserves left upon which to draw, and lamentably inadequate spiritual resources.

Football stars and show-business personalities receive immense adulation. Politicians, swollen with laughable self-importance, behave as if they have the word of life. But these new gods are not a patch on the old ones. An air of triviality and superficiality characterizes daily life, and it is enough to make the heart bleed. We have rejected religion, and sleep while the dark powers – which seem, often, to be inter-linked and highly organized – attack in a host of different guises. England, awake! The religion we have rejected could have offered, if handled with maturity, our best chance of countering these forces which, unchecked, could yet destroy much of what we cherish most. Is it too late?

There was never a golden age. Any such suggestion is romanticism run riot! Yet, until recently, there was *something* – and the cynics and the deniers must no longer go unchallenged. We spoke the same language; we acknowledged common points of reference. We believed in live-and-let-live; we believed in fair play, and – while we may not always have practised it – we admired honesty. We saw our pubs and our churches as part of Olde England; we respected and honoured the sovereign. A kind of mutual recognition – evident most recently, perhaps, during the Second World War – acted as the mortar which cemented society together. It has crumbled. Those who dismiss these remarks scornfully with the jibe that they represent simply the longings of a middle-aged man for a return to his boyhood in the '40s and '50s are, I think, mistaken. There can never be a going back. It is today and tomorrow which matter, and which fill me with concern. For we are a nation which has lost its way. England needs pointing-up, urgently, with a strong, fresh bonding. Where is it to be obtained? I believe with all my heart that, far above all else, England needs a religious revival.

4

The Revival of Wonder

I speak as a member of the Christian church when I affirm that England needs a revival of religion. It is Christianity I long to see rediscovered, stimulating the minds and imaginations of our countrymen. But I value and respect every gentle and sincere religious impulse. Any expression of devotion or wonder, and any attitude of reverence or compassion I welcome as a small sign of hope in what has become a very barren wilderness.

Recently, a church situated on a busy main road displayed prominently, on a poster, this message: 'My sincere beliefs are no substitute for the truth.' If the purpose of these 'wayside pulpits' is to stimulate thought, this was a great success, as far as I personally was concerned. Unfortunately, I rejected the sentiment – instinctively, intuitively, and instantly. It radiated a kind of arrogance which I found nauseating. I accept, of course, that it is easy to be sincerely wrong. Sincerity is not everything. Many fanatics have been sincere – and have performed terrible deeds. But without sincerity there can be no truth. And I honour the sincerely-held beliefs of every person who takes time and trouble to brood over the issues of life that really matter. Indeed, I ask of them nothing more. Eager as I am to share my own thoughts and experiences and convictions, we cannot force others to reach conclusions which harmonize more closely with our own opinions. Neither should we try. There is no way in which we can meaningfully advise people to put their sincere beliefs to one side and choose 'the truth'. It is a nonsensical play upon words. Their sincerity is the essence of their response to God – the 'Truth' at the heart of all things – and their very inability to embrace our views their testimony to that Truth.

The wise person is mindful, above all, that our present

understanding is necessarily fragmentary and incomplete. St Paul observes: 'For now we see through a glass darkly'. But if we are true to those glimpses of understanding which presently we possess, eventually more light and truth will dawn upon us, as our knowledge and experience grows. And nothing is more important than sincerity in the quest. If a person's sincerity is not good enough for us, we are indeed hard to please. My sincere beliefs *are* the truth, as far as I am able to perceive it at this moment.

It is, of course, the definition of 'truth' which is all-important: and the implication of the poster message was embarrassingly obvious. Trumpeted openly in the High Street, it conveyed an impression not of strong confidence but of smug superiority. 'It is we, in the church, who alone possess the truth.' That was the message of that poster. 'And the truth we possess is superior to your sincere beliefs.' That is a big claim to make and, to me, a very doubtful proposition. It generates incredulity and resentment. It has, in my view, nothing to do with 'I am the Way, the Truth, and the Life.' It is a graphic illustration of how language is used in different ways by different people on different occasions.

Within the church, the word 'truth' stands pre-eminently for the revelation of God which, we believe, we have received in Christ. But this is knowledge of a particular kind: it is 'religious knowledge'. And to use that same word 'truth', in a context specifically directed to the general public, and to suggest casually that we possess knowledge inherently superior to the sincere beliefs of the man in the street, smacks of pride and almost beggars belief. It comes dangerously near to conveying a profoundly irreligious spirit – just the kind of attitude, in fact, I am *not* anxious to encourage. The church has positive, creative, stimulating, even provocative messages of hope to share – but the last thing we should want to do is to disparage the sincere beliefs of others.

> The bruised reed he will not break;
> And the smoking flax he will not quench.

These considerations are particularly relevant to the fact that we live in a multi-faith society. The religious insights of other faiths should always be respected with warm and deferential tolerance, and with intense gladness that fellow human beings are not content to interpret their humanity simply in terms of crude materialism. We should not reluctantly tolerate – we should live in the earnest hope that we ourselves might learn and benefit from these other religions – that they might share, with us, some of their treasure. For, ultimately, there can be but one Truth.

However, the traditional and historic faith of England is Christianity. Its buildings dominate our cities and countryside and its heroes are part of our nation's story. It is the religion which has made England the fair land it is, and it is to Christianity I refer when I speak of our need of revival. Immediately, a direct and obvious question arises: What would a religious revival do for the people of England?

The first thing it would do would be to set our lives – our daily work, our thinking, and every experience – in their true context: the lofty setting of mystery and wonder. No other single factor would affect modern society so overwhelmingly. It would challenge our lazy new assumptions, restore our lost sense of proportion, and adjust our perspectives. Put bluntly, a religious revival would make us stop pretending that we are the lords and masters of this show – and such self-awareness would be good, for us and for the planet. For it is precisely at this point that we have most seriously lost our way.

Religion raises our sights above the trivial superficiality of our everyday concerns – where we plan, argue, and talk as though we shall live for ever – to a tantalizing, haunting realization that we are creatures of mystery. It enhances our stature by recalling us to fundamentals. It removes the mental, emotional and spiritual cataracts we have grown, uncovering and revealing afresh, like a newly-discovered wall-painting, our identity, and our predicament.

Religion reminds us that we shall die: that we are transient beings, one inter-related species among millions, forming an integral part of a living, moving, ever-changing cosmos. Yet we also possess intellect, music, hopes, dreams, visions and insights, which not only distinguish and set us apart from creatures but fill us with aspirations, longings, feelings, and thoughts extraordinarily difficult to identify and categorize. And, ultimately, of course, they defy adequate expression. We lose our train of thought . . . something distracts our attention . . . an idea, which came to us like a revelation, vanishes as suddenly, leaving us cheated, empty and dissatisfied, trying desperately to reach beyond its vague reflection and retrieve it, in the way we try unsuccessfully to recapture the details of a lost dream as it hurtles relentlessly away from us, back whence it came. Or we become bored; or tired; or our more primitive appetites prevail! But the capacity remains – the capacity to possess and pursue an 'inner life' – mental, emotional, spiritual – which augments and transfigures our animal nature. Sometimes we are exalted; often we are cast down; but frequently, we find within ourselves a curiously wistful spirit. Therefore, having addressed our mortality (relentlessly and unsparingly), religion proceeds to fire our dreams! It provides language, symbolism, and opportunities to acknowledge, express, and interpret all the distinctive elements of human experience (among which our fleeting experiences of 'holiness', reverence, and wonder are not least . . .)

A kind uncle bought me a second-hand bicycle when I was fortunate enough to pass the unlamented 11-plus examination, and I cycled miles, with boyhood friends, exploring the Norfolk countryside. With the possible exception of finding, in a field, an old bus being used as a store-shed or caravan, we liked nothing better than to peer into the village church, and to experience its awesome, slightly scary silence, and those smells produced by polish, damp, candles, and flowers. Not that we were noticeably religious. Sunday school had bored me to distraction. For too long it had represented the nadir of the week. Forty-five years later, I can recall my infant outrage at being expected to sing:

> Lord Jesus hath a garden, full of flowers gay,
> Where you and I can gather nosegays all the day:
> There angels sing in jubilant ring,

> With dulcimers and lutes,
> And harps, and cymbals, trumpets, pipes,
> And gentle, soothing flutes . . .

To me it was mostly unintelligible; the rest was nonsense! Sundays were a bit of a trial at the best of times – but what a way to spend an afternoon! I wanted to play in the shed with the boy next door, or watch the coaches go through to Yarmouth, or look for conkers (in the autumn) or birds' nests (in the spring). (I would very much have liked to play football in the alley, but that wasn't permitted on Sunday.) I left at the first chance and Sunday afternoons became popular opportunities for bike rides. Without guilt, we left Jesus to gather his own nosegays, while we headed out to the Norfolk Broads.

So we were not children given to religious excess. But this was something different: something real, almost tangible, and requiring no explanation. It was, of course, my first introduction to 'holiness'. And it was essentially intuitive. I knew how to behave in church, as distinct from Sunday school. Though none of us came from churchgoing families, we all knew. Churches were places for quiet and stillness. You didn't run about, or shout. Words like 'reverence', 'awe' and 'mystery' were not forever on our lips, but they summarize what we experienced – and we didn't know how lucky we were.

For it's gone. This ability to sense 'otherness' has been dissipated in a generation – just one example of the many ways in which the children of today are being robbed by having their childhood violated and filched from them.

I have had the custodianship of a mediaeval church for a quarter of a century, and had endless opportunities of observing children on school visits and other occasions. I realized, long ago, that today a very large number of them simply do not know how to behave in church. They have no perception of the church being essentially different from the other historic buildings they visit.

The fault could be mine. Perhaps if I prayed in the church more frequently and more fervently, I would contribute to the creation of a more powerful atmosphere of sanctity and devotion to which not even today's teenagers could remain impervious. In fact, the church already possesses a vibrant 'atmosphere'. In the morning and at evening it is particularly powerful. I believe sincerely that, as a child – with cycle clips on, pocket note-book bulging with bus numbers, and with a healthy curiosity about human sexuality equal to that of any youngsters of today – I would have sensed it instantly. I would have turned the great door handle slowly, in order not to make a noise; I would have crept in, perhaps even tip-toed; whispers and hushed tones would have been the order of the day. The consequences of any other demeanour were too dire even to think about.

Times change, and often for the better. Today's young people are more mature and worldly-wise than ever I was. Being reared in the age of instant telecommunication, they could hardly be otherwise. But there are losses, too, and these have not occurred suddenly. They have been creeping up on us for some time. Not all the teachers seem entirely at home in church, either.

This particular loss is eminently understandable, but frankly terrifying. If people don't really believe in God, or if they don't want to go very often to church services, that's their affair. I can handle that. I feel not dissimilar myself, sometimes. But not to recognize, or 'feel', what a church building represents – that it is a place for quiet reflection, for wonder, for thinking deep thoughts – that *is* depressing, and deeply disturbing. Religious rites and church buildings exist for us to express, however imprecisely, those vital attitudes to which I have already referred: awe, wonder, reverence, mystery. Many today are not familiar with creeds and dogmas, but these other experiences represent a fundamental element in what it means to be a human being. This strand of human consciousness is already seriously weakened. The city lights blot out the magic of the stars. But when we cease to wonder we become, paradoxically, less than fully human. The abandoning of religion – far from being a sign of our growing-up and coming-of-age – is, in fact, a dehumanizing process and it has begun.

Swollen with pride, we strut like little gods, imagining the entire cosmos to be under our control. But we are not gods. We are dependent creatures, and part of something greater. We appear; we exist for a moment in time, suspended in mystery; then we are gone. That is the reality. Yet it takes a gale, a storm, a flood, or a bereavement to remind us.

If our thinking is so flawed at this elementary level, what hope is there? Very little, unless we recognize the problem and address it with vigour and vision. Not that any of this is really new. It is much like the attitudes of Adam and Eve in the garden, who wanted to be God's equals. What is new, however, and threatening, is the scientific ability now at the disposal of our proud hearts. No wonder I watch the children in church anxiously.

But there are other reasons, too, why we should be anxious. The phenomenon which I, as a churchman, describe as the religious, worshipping impulse – the attitude which has its roots in the dramatic and the mysterious – is so utterly central to our being that if it is perpetually frustrated and denied, it will assuredly find unworthy and perverted expression. In this respect, it is remarkably similar to our sexual instincts which, if endlessly unacknowledged and repressed, will eventually be denied no longer, but break out and assert themselves, sometimes with disastrous consequences.

The horrifying case of the two youths from Canning Town who murdered a minicab driver, Fiaz Mirza, not long ago, contained one incidental but highly-significant detail. Suffice to relate that the crime was callous and merciless. Immediately after they had committed it, the two men called another cab which took them to Upton Park, the home of West Ham United football club. The former club captain, Bobby Moore, had died recently of cancer, and a memorial shrine had been erected at the ground. The young men who had just taken, in cold blood, the life of a good and kind man laid two little teddy bears dressed in West Ham colours beside the Bobby Moore shrine. Then they walked home.

The incongrous picture of brutal murderers employing little teddy bears in a quasi-religious activity is instructive. Notwithstanding their lack of personal morality, they needed symbols and gestures with which to express matters about which they *did* care. Lighting a candle and saying a prayer . . . or dressing up, in club colours, a little teddy bear . . . You can take your pick. But both attitudes stem from the same root. One action, however, retains an overt religious content which would normally preclude a vile, racist attack; the other was essentially trivial and emanated from minds from which religion evidently had been excluded, all fellow-feeling blunted, and which saw merit in murder.

Life is infinitely mysterious. It is unsolicited, unjust, full of beauty and pain, passes quickly, and ends in death. It is, ultimately, all beyond our control. This mysteriousness needs to be faced and given expression and recognition, otherwise our perspective fails and we become a danger to ourselves and to others. Religion enables us to do it. Excluding religion does not mean the mysteriousness will go away. Its repression will merely drive it inwards, in a thoroughly unhealthy fashion. Again and again, it will break out in ways ranging from the threatening to the infantile, from black magic, the occult and Nuremburg rallies, to drugs, hero-worship and teddy bears in claret and blue.

Although we experience mystery, awe and 'otherness' in a wide variety of forms, all stem from the same source. Ignorance is not the source, though a humble recognition of the limitations of human intellect is certainly part of it. The source lies in an instinctive awareness that we are creatures, not the Creator, and inhabit a multi-dimensional cosmos in which a great deal happens without our knowledge, consent, or participation. I selected the atmosphere of old churches and holy places to illustrate the way we experience reverence and wonder, but similar encounters are possible in endlessly different circumstances. For many, it is the majesty, beauty, energy and splendour of the natural world which most readily affects, excites and overwhelms them.

One May morning, I made a special effort to hear the dawn chorus. I climbed out of bed before half-past three, when the alarm clock rang, and made my way through dark and deserted streets, up to the heath. Blackbirds and thrushes were already greeting the day, and by five minutes past four a steady flow of bird-song was in progress. The sky was brightening in the east, but the woods were still dark; cockerels were crowing in the distance, and rabbits scampered away at my approach. Pheasants and wood pigeons added their distinctive calls, and at a quarter-past four – when the chorus swelled to its greatest volume and variety – I heard the cuckoo. I was astonished and moved to realize that this dramatic sound was spreading westward across the country.

I stopped spellbound when I heard the beautiful quavering hoot of a tawny owl; after a moment, an answering cry came from a different direction. I listened for two minutes; then, as owls and cuckoos called together, I decided it was light enough to enter the wood. Picking my way carefully through the gloom, I found one of the owls, silhouetted, and perched on a branch a few feet above me. Its head swivelled to look in my direction, but it continued to hoot, and its unseen companion continued to reply. I was utterly enchanted.

Soon after half-past four it was daylight. The darkness retreated, and the sky, in the east, was flushed with rose. I could hear chiffchaffs and willow warblers – but, already, the full chorus was over. As day broke, I marvelled at the fresh green of the larch, the catkins on the silver birch, the crab-apple blossom, and the gorse in full, golden flower. The world looked fresh and clean. It was Monday morning. The sun came up as I walked home marvelling that this drama – or something like it – occurs every day . . . and, unmindful, we sleep on. A long day stretched ahead, so I returned to bed at half-past five. When I awoke at eight, the memory of my visit to the heath seemed like a beautiful dream.

It is not only in the stillness of churches, or even when kneeling at the altar to receive the blessed sacrament, but also in experiences of this nature that my soul is renewed and revitalized. Amid the sights, scents and sounds of that daybreak I absorbed an energy, a deep draught of cosmic power, which replenished my spiritual resources, and recharged the batteries of my personality. It was an experience of darkness and light, a recognition of a rhythm of life which proceeds without our concurrence, or our conscious participation, yet to which we are inseparably joined. It was an acknowledgment of that ultimate relationship – our relationship, as creatures, to the cosmos – which by our forgetfulness and our delusions of self-sufficiency, we deny and bury beneath the superficialities of modern living. How pathetic we are, in our arrogance and in our slumbering!

When, at the cry of a bird, I entered that darkened wood, it was to offer worship, and to consummate a union with the energy throbbing powerfully through the soil, the sky, and the creatures. I wanted to confess and express my oneness with everything taking place around me. I wanted the energy behind the morning to vibrate and throb in *me* in every part of my body, and in my mind, and in those deepest recesses of my being of which I am scarcely aware, and to which I can give no name. My visit to the heath was no study-outing or holiday adventure. It was pre-eminently a religious experience. It may not have soared to mystic heights, nor plumbed unfathomable depths, but it was a *religious* experience, nonetheless, valid and primitive and potent, and the kind of religious encounter which is possible every day.

I could provide endless examples in a similar vein, from evening illustrations (of sunsets and afterglows, nightjars and moonlight) to experiences of pure wonder and delight (such as watching a privet hawk moth emerge, transfigured, from its chrysalis; or holding a grand-child). Each day produces moments of insight, mystery, and revelation – if our hearts were only attuned to receive them. Not many of these moments occur during church services, but when they do, they are likely to be particularly powerful.

At a church service I attended, one Sunday in summer, I sat behind four youths who were visiting the area on holiday. They were dressed very casually, but I observed that they followed the proceedings with care, kneeling for the prayers, bowing at the name of Jesus, and devoutly making the sign of the cross. I found this combination of holiday attire and religious devotion affecting and reassuring. Amid their holiday-making, they had still found time for the Great Acknowledgment (which is, ultimately, the meaning of worship). Afterwards, for all I know, they might have gone out and got tight or engaged in all manner of high-spirited antics (although I have no reason to think they did, apart from the fact that they looked young and energetic, and young men are prone to do those kind of things!). Suddenly, considerations of that kind didn't seem to matter very much. Their priorities were right.

Churchgoing is out of favour. In the eyes of many, it is an occupation for the weak and the weird. But in my book, nothing makes a youth more manly, or a young girl more mature, than to be found in an attitude of prayer and devotion. It is the 'missing link' of modern life: the antidote to our delusion of self-sufficiency. Football and cars and courting all have their rightful place; but to kneel, and to join in religious observance, is to acknowledge openly that the ultimate issues are not in our hands. It is a confession that mankind – for all his beauty and achievement – it is not absolute, but dependent. Such knowledge and humility are marks of spiritual stature. And it is precisely that spiritual stature which our generation has forfeited. Our technological and scientific abilities advance at breakneck speed – yet we have neither form nor language to express our fleeting religious instincts; and – because there is no stillness in our hearts – we fail to notice, or be affected by, the stillness in the church. Let me not beat about the bush! The English have become a race of spiritual pygmies!

I face an impossible task! I am writing about something which, ultimately, is intangible. So, at the risk of labouring the point, I will make one last attempt to convey the nature of my unease and concern. The words that follow are not mine, but are taken from one of the loveliest letters it has ever been my privilege to receive, and which was written in response to an article I had contributed to a newspaper.

Your article made us think of other things. It immediately called to mind a beloved botany teacher, who handled all living things with a gentle reverence that we could almost *see* as she showed us a flower or a plant, and described it to us. It reminded us of the wonder of lifting the lid of a shining new paint-box, or stroking the dust-jacket of a beautiful new book, as yet unopened on Christmas morning. It called to mind the deep hush of the school library, and the public library – places where one would not *dream* of breaking the silence – even the peace of the mobile library van, where people spoke in muted whispers. Nowadays it is a gossip shop!

We remembered the many cathedral closes throughout England which we have visited, and revelled in their ageless calmness and peace – and the lovely abbeys and priories, many of them ruined now, whose precincts still evoke reverence and quietness of mind and body. And, as we grow older, we appreciate the quietness of our own home and garden: the peace and fragrance of the herb garden; the arch of stars over the back porch at night, just before bedtime. We feel that people are much the poorer for no longer appreciating this dimension in their lives. My headmistress used to read a prayer in assembly which contained these words: 'We give thanks, O God, for the gift of wonder and the joy of discovery.' In our childhood, these were part of life. Not any more, we fear.

I cannot view this loss with equanimity. Too much is at stake. It is the reason I say: 'England needs a revival.' For this vital dimension of human experience, so basic and fundamental, would be the first to be reinvigorated by the revival of religion. I am *not* extolling ignorance, or advocating superstition – that much, at least, I hope I have made plain. But upon this aspect of our nature and being rests our health, our self-knowledge, and – ultimately – the well-being of the planet, our home. Without reverence, wonder, and marvelling; without an awareness of our smallness and dependence; without an instinctive affinity with the creation, and affection for its creatures great and small, there is nothing before us but disintegration and disaster. Read the signs of the times.

5

Fruits of Revival

The second thing a revival of religion would do for the people of England would be to provide a stimulating source of moral guidance. No one can doubt it is sorely needed. While millions have remained blissfully unaware (though others have grown vaguely uneasy) our moral values have been evaporating. This unhappy process has left the words 'right' and 'wrong' invested with less meaning and content that at any time in our national history. Obviously, this loss is as grave as the loss of our ability to experience awe, reverence, wonder and worship – indeed, the two are connected.

In the first instance we have forgotten how to treat the creation, and have lost our awareness of being part of a living, moving, mysterious creation: part of something infinitely greater than ourselves. In the second, we have forgotten how to treat one another: have lost the sense of being part of a community, of belonging together and being members of one another.

Here is a people with no urge to pray, no time to marvel, no patience with tradition, no reverence for the ancient holy places, no feeling for the changing seasons, no ability to pick out the constellations, no wonder at the mystery of their own being, and no quietness in their hearts. This same people view manners and old-fashioned courtesies as outmoded, regard each other primarily as competitors and rivals, and are prone to despise the poor. In their prosperity, they show little thought for the wider community and the well-being of others. Indeed, on one recent and celebrated occasion, the more lowly members of society were deemed gullible enough to be instructed that the true significance of the parable of the Good Samaritan lay in the fact that he actually had some money – not that there was kindness in his heart, even towards someone who might reasonably be thought to have had no claim upon him apart from his humanity and his need.

How can such a nation flourish and find greatness?

There is a tragic inevitability about it. If people – and especially young people – never hear the parable of the Good Samaritan, or the Sermon on the Mount, or any of the other inspired moral teachings contained in the Bible, they will lose touch with those traditional Christian values which – for all our failings – have for centuries provided the nation with a common moral language. Any terms of reference they possess today are just as likely to have been gleaned from elsewhere. I like to think that I have a remarkably open mind for one committed to the teachings of Christ, yet I am not persuaded that much is on offer of an inherently superior value. The Christian ethic of self-sacrificial love represents the loftiest heights of moral insight.

This lack of a set of generally-acknowledged moral values leads, first, to confusion and then to social disintegration. The process can be detected already. It can be seen in personal behaviour. There is nothing like the same emphasis on honesty, integrity, respect for others (especially our elders), 'fair-play', courtesy, chivalry, and care for the weak, which existed not long ago – the roots of which were all to be found in Christianity.

In social attitudes, recent changes have been both dramatic and appalling. An alien spirit of uncaring has seeped into our affairs, and although many continue to pay lip-service to old ideals, their actions belie their words. New attitudes have been engendered and stimulated by appeals to our most base and ignoble characteristics. Emphasis upon initiative, innovation, and enterprise – all admirable and much needed virtues, particularly when exercised in the service of the community – has been slanted to spawn a selfishness so gross as to be literally shocking. So great has been the impact that, without doubt, the national character has been affected – and in a manner which occurs only rarely. The community-spirit which existed amid

the dangers and deprivations of the Second World War and its
immediate aftermath (the period of my childhood) was the last
time something similar occurred. But the present sea-change in
attitudes has been in precisely the opposite direction.

In our brave new world, the effects of our actions upon others
– who may be less strong, less prosperous, less 'successful', or
less materialistic than ourselves – are simply ignored. Our
single-minded energy, guile, ingenuity, wealth and (not infrequently) unscrupulousness, are directed towards the goals we
desire personally, and the weakest can go to the wall. If there
are casualties, it is their own fault! They shouldn't be old/
young/poor/untalented/conscientious/or sick. This spirit is a far
cry from the England of not so long ago.

This political swing to the right, which has bitten so deeply
into the nation's sense of community, is based upon a lie and a
dangerous delusion. It is one of the cleverest and most cruel
political tricks: the offering to the majority of what only a
minority can ever conceivably enjoy. Yet the bait has been
taken. When spiritual reserves are low, the spirit of discern-
ment is one of the first casualties. Material expectations are
high. And people forget that if everyone could stand atop the
pile, there would be no pile.

A shop steward of long experience sat squarely before me, in
the canteen, and surprised me with the vehemence with which
he declared that we were in trouble. He was referring neither to
the union nor the company, but to the nation. His concerns
were wide-ranging, and embraced some of the matters to which
I have referred. His conclusion was that a moral vacuum existed
in the country from top to bottom; moreover, it would take
more than a change of government – which he fervently
desired! – to reverse the trend and change people's outlook.

This uncharacteristic and almost evangelical fervour thrilled
and impressed me deeply. The nation needs fresh moral
reserves – it is obvious to every thoughtful person of goodwill,
irrespective of creed or denomination. But who will supply
them; and from whence can they be obtained? A revival of
religion could supply them! Common ideals, a common
language, common terms of reference, values of compassion

and integrity – these would be the invaluable by-products of a new reverence and a new religious awareness throughout the land.

It is of vital importance to stress that both the benefits which would flow from a fresh emphasis on the significance and centrality of religion are not necessarily, in themselves, 'religious' in a narrow or sectarian sense. Those possessing no religious convictions, or with no liking for dogma, need not turn away and give up the quest before they have even begun. Everything I have tried to say in these pages hinges upon this realization – that religion itself, properly understood, and our desperately urgent need, are both greater than the demands of any specific denomination, sect or creed. I may here be skating on thin theological ice, but it will bear my weight; of that I have no doubt. The sense of wonder and mystery, and the golden rule of love, are two incomparably life-enhancing, humanizing experiences. As rational creatures, set in a universe of inexpressible complexity, it is necessary that we learn the humility which enables us to sense holiness, to experience wonder, and to admit we know so little. And, as moral beings, we need guiding principles to which, as a nation, we can give a common and unifying consent: No concept more noble than the love of one's neighbour, which lies at the heart of Christian teaching (and, in practical terms, means tenderness, compassion, humility, self-sacrifice, and justice), has been encountered in our long history.

Reverence and compassion; both would flow from a revival of religion, for both represent profoundly 'religious' attitudes, by any meaningful definition of the term. Yet neither necessarily involves commitment to any particular system of beliefs, nor intellectual assent to specific doctrinal propositions. This may be a bitter pill to swallow for some fervent believers, but the sooner we summon the courage to do so, the better. For 'religion' is a topic altogether larger than we have become accustomed to imagining. Think of it as three great circles, pushed together in a triangle, like snooker balls in a frame. The first two circles I have described already. I have now the embarrassing duty of having to tell all sincere disciples of 'organized religion', in any form, that they are crammed together in the third circle! I tell non-believers that the non-doctrinal aspects of life (which, nonetheless, come under the heading and umbrella of religion, properly understood) out-number the specifically doctrinal by two to one! They have a stake in two thirds of the territory covered by religion if they care and wonder about the mystery of the universe, and if they care and wonder about the mystery of humanity – even if they never lift another prayer book in their lives! This is the greatness of religion which we need, so urgently, to recognize. Religion must be wrested from 'the religious'! It involves so much more than hymn-singing, which is far from being everyone's cup of tea! It is about wonder and humanity before it is about institutional piety. Nobody should allow themselves to be put off by the word 'religion'. It is about our attitude to the cosmos, and to each other, before it is about church, mosque or temple.

Once that basic truth has been established, I am more than ready to concede and affirm that the practice of any brand of main-stream Christianity – any worthy activity within the third circle! – quickens and adds content to those two other expressions of true religion. Our sense of wonder, reverence, and mystery is enhanced; and our commitment to our neigh-bour, in both personal and social relationships, is intensified. The three faces of religion are at their most powerful when they are inter-linked. They belong together. But there is nothing automatic about it, which is why I have been at such pains, not only to separate them, but to put them in the right order. It is perfectly possible to fill every day with church activities and not to notice, still less be moved by, the changing seasons. It is manifestly easy to go to church regularly and to vote unhesi-tatingly for political parties which favour the well-to-do. So often, the practice of religion gives real religion a bad name.

It is, of course, possible to define words so widely that they lose their meaning, and some may accuse me of employing the word 'religion' in that fashion. For reasons which by now I hope, are apparent, I would not only deny the charge: I would maintain that our customary failure lies in the opposite direction. We define 'religion' too narrowly, and seem to imagine we've captured God in a bottle. But the God of the scriptures cannot be confined, contained, or tamed. The God to whom the Bible testifies is a boundless, fertilizing energy, permeating, burning, sweeping through all creation, sometimes as a rushing, mighty wind; sometimes as a still small voice. Those who think the third circle is the only circle have a lot to learn. They could begin with evidence to be found within their own sacred scriptures, which lie at the heart of Christian belief and practice. The existence of the first circle is suggested movingly in the picture of the psalmist under the spell of the night sky, contained in Psalm 8:

> When I consider thy heavens, the work of thy fingers, the moon and the stars, which thou has ordained: What is man, that thou art mindful of him?

That blend of wonder, reverence, mystery, humility and awe lies at the very heart of true religion, and millions who never set foot in church buildings would still be able to recognize the experience described by the psalmist, and identify with it. Religion is natural to us; it is in us all.

The existence of the second circle, representing our moral responsibility for one another, and an indication of its precedence over the third, is indicated clearly in the Sermon on the Mount:

> If thou bring thy gift to the altar, and there rememberest that thy brother hath ought against thee; leave there thy gift before the altar, and go thy way; first be reconciled to thy brother, and then come and offer thy gift.

There is much more in the same vein in the epistle of James.

Some may find it unusual that a minister of the gospel should write in these terms, but I have spent my ministry in the English mission field, exposed and buffeted, never cushioned or protected. I have lived where many of the words and concepts which are so precious and meaningful to us when we use them in church convey no meaning whatsoever. I have been forced to define, and re-define, in attempts to convince people not only that I live on the same planet and speak the same language, but that religion is a subject of interest and importance. I have urged that far from being the preserve of the childish or the quaint, it actually merits their attention, because it wrestles with fundamental issues. I have had to try to persuade people that they themselves are, in fact, religious creatures, and that most of them have had religious experiences. I have been utterly sincere in my insistence – to them, so novel – that their non-churchgoing religious experiences (in the trenches, on the mountain, on a negotiating committee, or watching a film) have been more profound than those given to many people who have devoted much time in the pursuit of activities more overtly religious. It's a silly way of speaking, I know, but to me it conveys the most valuable insight given since my teenage conversion: God spends two-thirds of his time at work *outside the church*!

But no parson worth his salt could ever leave it there! All who are deeply immersed in the life of the Christian church – whatever their denominational brand – will be impatient at this low-key approach to the benefits of religion, and rightly so! The third circle is packed with treasure beyond description and without price. A revival of religion would not only set our lives in the true context of wonder and mystery; it would not only provide a source of moral guidance and an ethic of compassion and integrity. The third benefit would be the offer of spiritual insight and experience through worship and devotion.

Many would argue, I know, that properly understood this third benefit embraces the previous two and, therefore, is the only one on which we need to concentrate! For those securely within the life of the church, this is certainly the case. The practice of the Christian religion produces sensations of wonder and holy joy equal to those provoked by the creation. And contemplation of the Divine Love, particularly in the sacrament of Holy Communion, releases a loving energy infinitely greater and more comprehensive than any formal ethic of love. That is the theory! And – Yes! – for countless thousands, it is the truth in deed and practice.

But religion itself – as distinct from the need to experience wonder, and the need to possess a common ethic and set of moral values (for both these are universal, and transcend all religious forms and practices) – is rather like a hobby. Some people find the subject credible, even fascinating; discover a vivid personal faith; actually *enjoy* singing hymns; and are generally content to commit much of their spare time to the cause. Others prefer tennis, politics or stamp collecting. The choice is theirs. God has made us different, and our varied gifts enrich our common life. I long to share the things which, to me, mean so much – above all my faith in Christ. And I am boisterous in my witness; yet I am hesitant, too, and would sooner remain silent than appear to inflict my personal beliefs upon a reluctant and unreceptive victim. Those days have long gone. When members of certain sects try it on me I become livid. There is, these days, an essential balance to be maintained between quiet, positive, affirmation, and anything that smacks of coercion or proselytism.

To those whose hobby is other than religion, I testify simply: there are good things waiting to be discovered in the church. There are ancient writings which burn their way into the heart; music which haunts; ideas which stimulate and provoke; a presence which defies analysis; and a peace which passeth all understanding. They are there if you want them. They are part of your national heritage. They are yours by right, as a human being. A revival of religion would make it easier for you to experiment and discover for yourself what is on offer. But the choice will always remain yours.

I certainly don't suggest people will go to hell if they remain unimpressed, neither do I comment adversely on their lack of interest. Their opinion is as valid as mine. But if they invite me to say more about my commitment to the Christian faith, I am eager and willing to oblige, sometimes picking my words carefully, sometimes flaunting the distinctive vocabulary of church, depending upon the audience. The mystery and the power of prayer; the ecstasy of worship at its noblest; the almost-tangible strength to be found in bread and wine; the delight of Christian fellowship and the communion of saints; the joy of the great festivals; the inspiration of sacred scripture; the boundless and uplifting world of hymnody; choral evensong; a sense of purpose; a sense of forgiveness; a mystical relationship of love with Jesus.

These are the things I treasure. This is what it means to me. In my case, Christianity and matters ecclesiastical are not a hobby. There have, I confess, been days when I've wished I had never encountered the church; but they have been black days. To me, religion is infinitely more than an interest. Christianity has become as integral a part of my being as breathing. And, despite my criticisms of the church, I do not speak as an impartial observer but as a disciple of Christ, committed to his way. It is from that viewpoint I reiterate my conviction that a revival of religion – a renewal of interest in religion, and a rediscovery of its potency – would transform the nation utterly. It would set human life in its true and mysterious context. It would supply values of integrity and compassion. And, for those willing to go further (once they could be half-convinced that a journey existed to be undertaken), it would open the door to life's vast spiritual dimension, and provide experiences of religion, glimpses of God, and a vibrant living faith.

A long list could be drawn up of changes which would enrich our national life. Our suggestions, no doubt, would vary according to our personal preferences. But nothing would release more vital energy, nor generate a more profound renewal, than a revival of religion. A rediscovery of her historic faith would re-invigorate England, cleanse and sweeten our common life, and release a great surge of revitalizing, creative energy. England needs a revival.

6

Reservations

Before we get carried away, however, it is time to express some substantial qualifications. England assuredly does not need *any* kind of religious resurgence. To be worthwhile: to be a blessing and a liberation rather than an expression of reaction, five factors, at least, need to be borne in mind.

The first and most important, can be stated bluntly. The religious revival our country needs cannot be based upon fundamentalist attitudes. The world needs more religious fundamentalism like it needs a hole in the head – and, when you think of it, the two often go together. I never tire of observing that idolatry takes many forms, and bibliolatry is one of the most insidious. Fundamentalism is utterly alien to the religion of the New Testament and its emphasis upon the Holy Spirit. Christianity is about the excitement of seeking, and of being led into all truth. It is not about having a holy book, containing all the answers, rammed down your throat. That may be putting things crudely and a little unkindly, but is it time for plain speaking.

You cannot, of course, love God directly without loving the sacred scriptures, which point to him and to our blessed Saviour. (You can love God *indirectly*, through nature, and through love for your neighbour, and love for your friends – but the rarest insights come from the book of God.) The Bible inspires, guides, chastens, challenges, and nourishes. 'Thy word is a lantern unto my feet: and a light unto my paths.' It is the eternal bedrock of meaningful Christian discipleship, a divine and priceless gift, and a unique instrument of the Holy Spirit. But it is not a compendium of ready-made answers. God simply does not work in that fashion. Like the wind, the Spirit bloweth where it listeth. To be able to quote endless strings of biblical verses proves nothing. It is possible to have a head full of texts and a heart full of hardness. Anyone who has fallen foul of the fundamentalist wing of God's legions will bear me out.

That particular brand of Christian discipleship is vociferous, zealous, and apparently in the ascendent. It is making converts. It is turning others away from religion for life. The catastrophic destruction by fire of the central and local history libraries of the city in which I live was described in a letter to the local newspaper as a God-given opportunity to dust down our Bibles and receive God's wisdom for a change, instead of depending heavily on man: 'Libraries? The Lord gives, and takes them away.' A few days later, a similar letter appeared, on the subject of school assemblies: 'The Bible is the most exciting book in the world today. It covers every subject in the school curriculum: history, geography, maths, English, poetry, adventure, romance, etc.' Thus an eagerness to say something genuinely worthwhile is marred by the extremely simplistic and sectarian tone of the observations which, usually, prove counter-productive. The credibility of the Christian faith is diminished, and those whose religion is of a nature quite different are nevertheless tarnished by the incredulity and ridicule these sentiments provoke.

The second letter continued: 'A few days ago I was speaking to a young man in his early twenties who said that until he was converted to Christianity, he believed in evolution because that was what he had been taught in school. I do not think this is an isolated case.' It is possible to counter these expressions of opinion with views that are, perhaps, more balanced and realistic. By then, however, the damage has been done. Our task (as I understand it) is to encourage attitudes of reverence, devotion, and obedience to the scriptures. The point which fundamentalists miss, however, is that the scriptures not only permit but positively encourage the exercise of that same critical scrutiny we bring to every other area of life. The cars we drive didn't drop from the sky, and neither did the Bibles we treasure. Cars and Bibles are part of the same world, made of the same chemicals, and products alike of disciplined and enquiring minds. (And my illustration, I feel, is well chosen. Some of those who idolize their Bibles most fervently tend – I have noticed – to be very fond of their cars, which are, not infrequently, new models! But I digress.) To men and women of faith, the same God is involved in the production and maintenance of cars and the development and interpretation of scripture. Both, therefore, should be subject to the same rigorous inquiry. There are not two categories of intellectual integrity. There is one truth.

Christians should not fear truth, from wherever it proceeds. If it is true, it is of God. Truth, of course, is multi-faceted. Faith and knowledge are equally valid responses to truth in its varied aspects; doubt and uncertainty are valid responses, too. In our handling of the scriptures, our reverence should mingle with the spirit of open inquiry; while all our questioning should be tempered with humility.

If we think we can convert England by the endless (and selective) recitation of scripture, we're in for a nasty shock. For every convert won, there will be twenty repelled and confirmed in their godlessness. And people like me will be tempted to join them – held back only by a sense of loyalty, and a sense of repugnance at handing over the church to the reactionaries and extremists. They must not be given the satisfaction. Instead, their blinkered, narrow vision must be exposed.

I used to discuss these matters in low-keyed, measured tones, believing myself to be the very essence of sweet reason. I no longer bother, but concentrate solely on telling it the way it is. As I grow older and begin to sense time running out, I no longer care about giving offence to people, who, in any case, ought to know better. In addition, the issues confronting our country and the church grow ever more urgent: too much mealy-mouthed 'niceness' is a luxury we can no longer afford. But beyond all this is the painful realization born of long experience that such efforts are usually a complete waste of time. There is nothing more inflexible than a heart gripped by religious fundamentalism. The proud, impertinent assumption that scripture can only be interpreted one way is repulsive; and the inability to translate the written word into a humble, reverent, tentative – yet vital – spirit of contemporary insight is the ultimate religious futility.

In an article I wrote for a religious magazine, I was incautious enough to reflect, ruefully: 'I think it likely I shall go to hell – but at least I won't go with clean hands.' It prompted a batch of hurt, puzzled, and angry letters. One woman handed me a leaflet containing a step by step guide on how to be saved. (Actually, it was rather a good leaflet. Forty years ago I would have found it interesting.) I grew tired of having to explain that my phrase was a kind of poetic licence, an imaginative or exaggerated expression, designed to emphasize a point, or to stimulate thought. It sprang in this case from a profound and abiding awareness of what I deserve. But there is a rigidity in certain brands of discipleship which seems to me a denial of everything the New Testament says and represents. In the rent-a-verse world of religious fundamentalism, there is no room for poetry, for irony, for imagination, for humour – and where there is no humour there is no God, for humour is about true self-awareness, and self-awareness reveals our laughable insignificance apart from God. Instead, there is only hardness of heart; just hardness of heart – and a book. But Christianity is about the spirit of compassion, the spirit of wisdom, the spirit of truth. It does not reside in a tome of ready-made answers. No such volume exists. By the very nature of the human race, with its inquiring mind and ever-accumulating experience, it cannot exist. What does exist is a sacred volume of unrivalled beauty and power, which testifies to Jesus Christ, and speaks with unique authority to hearts and minds alike. For two thousand years it has nourished, stimulated, inspired, informed, converted. It is the sceptre with which Christ rules his church; it is certainly no man's plaything. But it is a source of liberty, not a fresh set of religious shackles.

I have a mental picture (which may be the remnant of a dream) of a circle of grim-faced people gathered around a large open Bible. In my imagining, they are all dressed in black. They are searching for a verse upon which to seize and interpret as a sign – possibly, even to use as confirmation of their own prejudices. It is a disagreeable and slightly sinister

picture – my own symbolic protrayal of religious fundamentalism. I have a second, contrasting picture, full of light and
laughter which do not for an instant detract from the solemnity
and sincerity of the scene. These men and women, too, are
exploring the scriptures diligently. But their spirit is different.
They are not looking for words which will clinch things, once
and for all. They are looking for words which speak to their
condition, which challenge, provoke, inspire, delight; words
which give them food for thought, and nourishment of a far
deeper kind. It is this second group of people who are in fact,
placing themselves most faithfully under the authority of the
Word of God, and letting the Bible speak. The first group –
despite their counter-allegations – are much more prone to
impose their firmly-held opinions on the Word. The second
group expects the Holy Spirit to use the sacred scriptures to jolt
and direct their thinking, and so bring them closer to understanding the will of the living God and the Risen Lord.

How dare the fundamentalists imply that their love of the
scriptures is greater than mine! And why are they allowed, so
often, to get away with their impertinence? I prove my
reverence for scripture by refusing to treat it as a puzzle game –
'Hunt the Text' – and by expecting it to work, in me, today –
quickening my thinking and deepening my devotion.

The ever-increasing practice of quoting the Bible to unbelievers, as if it were self-evidently self-authenticating, is
illogical and therefore usually unproductive – certainly among
those who retain their critical faculties. Peddling verses is not
our task, as we strive to promote a revival of true religion. What
we should be doing is teaching people who are theologically
challenged how to handle religious myths, to prevent them
throwing out the baby of genuine religious insight with the bathwater of fundamentalist nonsense. Christianity is based upon
lots of dramatic stories, or myths, many of which are interpreted historically; some are apocalyptic (visionary and symbolic),
while others have origins lost in the mist of time. Together,
these religious myths help us to handle, and cope with, the
realities of the day – a bereavement or a birth, a morning or an
evening, a disappointment or a temptation, a mid-winter

celebration or a festival of spring. The great value of a myth is
that it will bear as much or as little weight as you care to put
upon it. It isn't a mere question of learning verses, though the
myths tend to stick vividly in the mind. It has to be thought
about, its meaning teased from it, its lessons learned and
applied. Tomorrow, you may interpret the myth differently.
You may believe more, or see things more clearly – or you may
discard some ideas as no longer credible and forming the husk
rather than the kernel. This flexibility is not discreditable.
Rather it is the mark of a vital and living faith. It is the joyful
secret of true discipleship which, paradoxically, is ever fixed
and grounded, yet never static. It rests upon the hypothesis of
the existence of an eternal God, and it rests upon the historicity
of Jesus of Nazareth: but it is fired by a contemporary Spirit
who, we are assured, will lead us into truth. Circumstances
change, we grow, the world alters. How we see things today
may not correspond with the way we shall see them tomorrow.
With fresh discoveries daily in every walk of life and in
ourselves, it would be unrealistic to look in the Bible for
detailed and practical solutions to questions which had not yet
been posed! Not even the most sacred scriptures could contain
them. But the stories, ideas and teaching which the Bible
contains are a source of endless stimulation and inspiration.
They touch our minds – not yesterday, but today – with a
mysterious freshness, potency, and creativity, which alter our
perspectives, raise our hopes, quicken our endeavours, and set
our lives in their true context. They make our thinking
pregnant with the possibility of God.

Those who have let the stories of the Bible slip from their
mind have lost an irreplaceable intellectual and emotional
resource, without which their lives are immeasurably the
poorer. Yet, despite that poverty, fundamentalist attitudes are
not the answer. To many, they are not only incredible; they are
an affront to integrity. But a fresh understanding of that daring
lightness of touch with which religious myth can be handled,
and a new experience of the light and liberty it produces, would
set the Bible once again at the heart of our national consciousness. Its words could be weighed in a rational, honest manner,

and without embarrassment. And England would be the sweeter.

If militant fundamentalists, and even those slightly less extreme in their approach to the Bible, fill me with despair, many modern atheists have an identical effect. People who know the lot have much in common with those who know there is nothing *to* know. The certainties and the absolute dogma of both groups chill my spirit, and leave me with a sense of heaviness, loneliness, and isolation. Fundamentalists or atheists – they know more than I know. For me, existence is a mystery, made bearable by the warmth of love and the tiny shafts of insight I have been granted: from music, from nature, and – not least – from the Christian myth and the faith of the church. But it is all very tentative, and alarmingly 'live'. Faith ebbs and flows and – in a sense which means a great deal to me, – just as the world is created new every morning, so I need to be converted afresh each day, too.

Neither those who have God neatly tied up (with chapter and verse to prove it), nor those strangely happy in the conviction that there *is* no meaning, speak to my condition. I pursue a quest which I take up anew, daily. Sometimes I feel I may have made a little progress; often, I know I am back at square one! It is possible to find, and then lose. And often, the place which one day seemed to be a destination looks only a staging post the next. There is always a beyond, a beckoning, a hunger which can sometimes be assuaged but never sated. So I continue to search, and hope that in seeking I am growing. For some discoveries I am overwhelmingly grateful, particularly for every fragment of knowledge about Jesus Christ, but the journey never ceases, neither does the hope that when we no longer see through a glass, darkly, I may be better equipped to understand a little more. Meanwhile, the search can be immensely invigorating. There is joy in the quest. Yet religious belief is not always easy; to pretend otherwise is a lie.

For most people, belief can never be easy. By the very nature of the case, we can never be certain, we cannot *know*, not in the common, everyday sense of the word. Indeed, it is obvious that we were not designed to know. When St Paul said: 'I know in whom I have believed,' it seems to me unlikely that he was using the word in the sense we employ when we affirm that we know our next-door neighbour, or know how to strip down and rebuild the engine of our motor car. If he *was*, one can only say that his experience was utterly and overwhelmingly different from our own; so different, in fact, that it casts a cloud over many of the other tremendous things he said. He was scarcely one of us! But I think he *was* like us. He was using 'know' in a distinctive and religious sense. He had journeyed along the Damascus road.

If a Supreme Being exists – the source of all being, the upholder, from moment to moment, of all creation and all worlds – that Being must be forever beyond our comprehension. One glimpse of such splendour would consume us. Instead of bemoaning our isolation, we should rejoice in the blessing of God's remoteness. A God we could 'know', as we know one another, would be a much more manageable force than the Ultimate Energy-beyond-and-within-all-things, incomprehensible and eternal, which most thoughtful nonchurchgoers (without training in philosophy or the meaning of language) regard as the only vaguely plausible kind of definition of Divinity. Forget the Oxford common room. I'm trying to give God a toe-hold in the canteen, and this sort of approach represents his best hope! Were the Archbishop of Canterbury himself to say that he *knows* God exists, eyebrows of sceptical disbelief wold be raised, my own among them. Language used in that fashion is barely meaningful outside the church. Yet there are a few prepared to acknowledge that God does exist – if only by definition! – not as an entity external to our universe and to our own being but as a force which creates and renews and nurtures it from within. That is our starting point.

If we yearn to see the Christian religion regain and retain its place at the heart of our national life, we must encourage people to understand that it is essential both to be at ease with religious myth and to maintain intellectual integrity. And why should it be always easy? Nothing worthwhile is ever easy! But that is the spirit in which we must travel. The key to making some progress lies in recognizing that words can and do mean

different things to different people at different times, and never
more so than in the realm of religion where, by definition, we
are dealing with the unknowable and inexpressible.

Funerals provide interesting illustrations of the religious
situation in England today. Those present have often no mature
understanding of what the church represents and offers, and
the result is a mixture of disbelief and embarrassment instead of
powerful, efficacious religion.

The 'average' congregation at a funeral will contain at least
three significant groups. Firstly, those who are able to take
every word of the proceedings more-or-less at face value.
Secondly, those who doubt whether any 'objective reality' lies
behind most of the liturgy. Many, however, accept the value of
the language and the myths (a) as vehicles for directing the
emotions in an ordered and cathartic manner and (b) as a
colourful expression of insights which have undeniable validity
and usefulness (for example, the centrality of love and self-
sacrifice to human happiness and fulfilment, and the applica-
tion of concepts like resurrection to everyday life and experience). Thirdly, those in between, who try hard to accept as
much as possible and respect even the bits they can't.

At funerals, the religious myth ennobles the proceedings and
lifts the spirit, equipping us to deal both with the enormity and
the futility of the occasion. Secular funerals are becoming more
common, and doubtless they are sometimes of the highest
standard. But my personal, limited experience of them has been
horrendous. Secular funerals risk leaving everybody grounded.
Their rigorous intellectual propriety frequently backfires, for it
is not as easy to construct a funeral rite as might be imagined.
Sometimes the attempt is brave and successful, but often, their
hopelessness and sense of finality comes near to denying
something vital and impossible to define, yet which belongs to
the very essence of our nature: that longing in the human spirit
to soar, to explore, to look, to reach ever beyond.

In a secular funeral, our wings are clipped. But the mention
of wings brings us dangerously close to the traditional myths, in
their starkest and most simple forms. If I am not careful, I shall
be mentioning harps next! But, then, what is human life

without music? Here, the atheist or secularist agrees. He will almost certainly include music in his non-religious rite (often, religious music!) But what is music for? What does it do? It helps the human spirit to express the inexpressible. It cuts through all material forms, and speaks direct to our inmost substance, our inmost being. It paints pictures, and prompts dreams, and whispers secrets that we can never share. In short, it challenges a narrow, materialistic interpretation of human life and experience, rather like religious myth, properly handled and understood.

It is not, then, only the fundamentalists who jeopardize the revival of true religion in England (although their contribution is frankly alarming). Other groups and attitudes also play their part. Indeed, between those who know it all, because it's been handed to us in a Book, and those who think we've made the whole thing up – an inverted fundamentalism, equally depressing – there is not much to choose.

Humble seekers after truth have many pitfalls to avoid. Yet it is between those poles we must attempt to steer our course if England is to rediscover its soul.

7

More Qualms and Qualifications

Other qualifications must now be mentioned. A revival of religion in England must embrace four ingredients, without which it would be better to have no revival, leaving religion as a gently-declining minority pursuit to take its chance with the dark forces arrayed against it.

The religious revival our country needs must be essentially catholic-spirited. It must leap over the historic denominational barriers which still divide us, but which have been long obsolete. Throughout my ministry I personally have ignored them, except to rejoice in the diversity of our heritage and experience. The *interesting* differences between Christians – which will always exist, pray God – cut across denominational lines and concern matters like our approach to scripture, worship and social issues.

The rejection of the Anglican-Methodist unity conversations by the Church of England, on two occasions early in my ministry, cast a shadow which has continued to blight the church's message and mission to the people of this land over the years that have followed. The moment came, and the moment was lost. Those of us who argued in favour of the scheme saw it as a heaven-sent opportunity. It was a chance to re-engage the national consciousness, to make people aware once more of our existence, and to speak to them the words we longed to speak and which they needed to hear. We believed that the consequences of failure would be grave and invite the judgment of God. Within the church's younger ranks (already bewildered and impatient at our divisions) we forecast disillusion; for the church's mission we forecast a crisis of uncertainty leading to a grinding halt; for the spiritual and moral life of the nation we forecast a continuing and unchallenged decline. The opponents of the proposals triumphed. The scheme, which had seemed to me so exciting and imaginative, sank without trace.

In 1982 the convenant proposals, in which the Free Churches were invited to take episcopacy into their system, seemed like God's second chance, given to help us put right the appalling mistake we had made. This scheme, too, was kicked into touch by the national church, to its great shame. Since the rejection of the Anglican-Methodist proposals, I have had little heart for inter-church committees and councils. I'm not proud of the fact – simply stating the truth. I was young and disheartened, and I believed the decision would make my ministry more difficult and less productive. I threw myself into it (as I shall describe), and left these other matters to those who still felt able to pursue them. Today, the received wisdom seems to be that the rejection of the Anglican-Methodist conversations was a blessing in disguise. It prevented serious splits in both churches, and brought us to the present situation in which there is unprecedented friendship and co-operation between the denominations. That is not my reading of the situation. I believed at the time that the defeat of the proposals was a historic disaster, for the church and for the nation. Today, I believe it even more.

Nobody can prove what would have happened if a different decision had been reached. Your guess is a good as mine! But I have the strongest conviction that both church and nation would have been in incomparably better heart. I suspect the country would have been spared the worst excesses of our recent history: the great surge of ruthless selfishness which all but swamped the nation; the weakening of the social ties that bind us in one community; the injustices, the hatreds, the despair. I believe that the union of the Church of England and the Methodist Church – the coming together of 'church' and 'chapel' – would have made an impact upon the life of the nation unparalleled in the modern history of the English church. Widespread and continuing publicity would have been guaranteed. The inter-availability of the ministries of both churches would have soon placed some Free Churchmen in novel and influential appointments. The traditional social witness of the Free Churches would have made itself noticed as never before. People would have been interested, and some would have wanted to become involved. The very spirit of England would have been sweetened by this great religious sign of hope – and we threw it all away! Our national church played at religion instead of acting with prophetic vision, courage and faith, and refused to seize the historic opportunity with both hands. The nation paid a heavy price. I do not expect to see a similar opportunity again in my lifetime.

Within the church itself, the consequences have been nothing short of disastrous. The chief victim has been public worship, which has sagged in quality and efficacy to a very low point. The worship of Almighty God is the prime reason for the church's existence; if we fail here, we fail completely. I am aware that to some, my tone will again sound offensively bilious, and I am striving truly to avoid that impression. I have described, however, how, since I have reached middle age, it seems more important than ever to me to speak the truth in love. In the past I have leaned over backwards particularly to avoid giving offence to Christians of a fundamentalist persuasion. I have realized only recently that sweet reason does not necessarily generate a similar response. Indeed, in that particular instance, it is like water off a duck's back! No meeting of minds takes place, and texts continue to be churned out regardless. It is time now to drop the pretence and expose dangerous, counter-productive nonsense for what it is; and time to speak about worship in the same blunt and honest way.

I am not bilious. I am remarkably relaxed. But I am sad, deeply and desperately sad. I never foresaw it would be this bad. An embarrassing spirit of triviality has invaded Christian worship in England today. Time and again, in the bearing of the preacher and the content of the liturgy, there is little to suggest the presence – let alone convey an experience – of the living God. The speed with which all sense of the numinous, all dignity, reverence and awe has been dissipated, in church and chapel alike, is scarcely credible. It jeopardizes our mission, because this ought to be one of the most precious gifts we have to offer. I attribute much of the blame to the failure of the Anglican-Methodist conversations.

It was obvious some twenty-five and more years ago. We needed each other, not for strategic missionary purposes alone, but for reasons linked closely to our worshipping and devotional life, without which we have and are nothing. Put simply, without abandoning our distinctive emphases and ethos, the Methodists of the twentieth century needed to tap more deeply into the devotional heritage of the catholic church while the Anglicans – saddled with one of the devotional classics of Christendom – needed to loosen their stays (or their gaiters or *anything*) and make a little more room for the Holy Spirit and the Risen Lord. What lovely things we could have done together! How we could have taught and shared with one another, not merely by having experts on each other's committees but by growing into each other's lives at local level, and utilizing the accumulated wisdom of that practical experience. We would have grown together *with understanding*, enriching and sharing with one another. But the evangelicals and the anglo-catholics lost their bottle. They didn't want it. They thought they didn't need it. An unholy alliance defeated and brought to nought the most exciting opportunity that has presented itself to the English church since the Reformation.

The changes, which were inevitable, have duly taken place. Methodist services have become more 'churchy', Anglican worship much less 'formal'. But, for all the consultation which has taken place, the changes have been essentially denominational: ASB for BCP, H&P for MHB. And where close fellowship and co-operation have encouraged more borrowing from each other (which is much to be applauded and encouraged), it has of necessity been unstructured and frequently without understanding. Methodist ministers, starved of that essential catholicism without which true religion shrivels, wear stoles and brightly coloured scarves on a gloriously ad-hoc basis. Chapels are redesigned to look like churches, frequently losing their distinctive and precious ethos as a result. Old identities are surrendered, but not replaced by anything of equal worth. Anglicans, meanwhile, have put 'And can it be?' at the top of their charts, but it is ceasing to send a chill up the spine, and seldom sounds like it used to in the chapel! Too often, the words are being sung without the experience. These illustrations are not intended to be taken too seriously, but they will serve to make the point.

What had to happen *has* happened. But we took the easy option, and settled for second best. We voted to avoid the pain, and landed ourselves in one terrible mess. Everything I write is, of course, a purely personal opinion: but take the work of liturgical revision. Not all of it has been done well. The modern translations, hymnals and service books will not save us. But the warmth of Methodism, poured into the heart of the Church of England, could have produced a quality of worship which spoke both to the mind and heart of our age. Instead, a terrible thing has happened. We have gatherings for worship, but we don't always have a God. Don't ask people like me! We still go to church every week. Ask those who step inside only on rare occasions. They will tell you. There's nothing there.

If true, where does that leave our mission to the nation? That question alone is bad enough. But of course it gets worse. Frequently, these days, there *is* something there. There is, for every level-headed, mature and self-respecting person, embarrassment! It awaits the unwary in the most astonishing and unlikely places. I am referring, of course, to the great lurch towards pentecostalism which has occurred over the same period. Each to their own! I believe utterly in religious tolerance and in freedom of speech and worship. Only those who advocate violence and incite hatred will find me an opponent. Those who find blessing in a fundamentalist form of religion, and those who delight in the various forms of pentecostalism have every right so to do, and God will surely bless those who tread these particular paths in sincerity, and seeking truth. But it is important to make clear that they do not represent the heart and substance of main-stream Christian tradition. It is equally important to understand that they do not typify the form of religious revival England desperately requires; and they most certainly do not – despite their present growing numbers – point in the direction that we should go, if we hope ever to see that day.

The overwhelming majority of the English will be roused spiritually only when their minds are meaningfully engaged also, not affronted. To say that is not to declare religious experience to be the product of unaided human thought. I, personally, most certainly do not think in those terms. What there must be, however, is a harmony between heart and mind which undiluted fundamentalism and dreamy-eyed, arm-waving pentecostalism undermines. Pentecostalism in modern Britain is a diversion. It has taken a greater hold because we said 'No' to Anglican-Methodist unity. That scheme alone would have enriched the spirituality of all who threw themselves into it with enthusiasm. The catholic traditions of the Church of England would have re-ignited the fires of Methodism. But 'the chapel' had plenty to offer too, though many were too proud to see it, or too ignorant. The experience of the warmed heart lies at the centre of Methodist worship. It is harder to define than to experience. But when the scriptures are expounded and the old hymns sung by those who know their meaning, it can be felt. And it is this warmth, this experience, this drop of spiritual reality which would have burned its way into the bones of the Church of England from top to bottom, and spoken of God. It would have done more than any other single factor I can imagine to re-equip the English church for its task of giving to the nation a Christian heart, Christian ideals, Christian vision and Christian experience. The creation of a more Christian society is our first goal, and small doses of pentecostalism are at best an irrelevance and at worst a grave distraction. It could all have been so different! All our efforts could have had so much more 'body', have been 'earthed' and potent and contagious. To some, of course, pentecostalism *is* contagious; but to most it is grossly off-putting and more than faintly ridiculous. And in some of its manifestations it is frankly alarming and potentially dangerous. It is not a million miles from the other varied forms of brain-washing practised by sects and cults from time immemorial and which seem to have come into their own in recent years, boosted by the new manipulation made possible by modern wealth, transport and telecommunications.

If I am not hostile to every expression of pentecostalist fervour, I am usually suspicious and extremely dubious. It seems to me so often to be forced, and to lack that sincerity and truth which undergirds religion at its highest. The nub of my dismay and anguish – made almost unbearable because so few seem able to recognize or share it – is the conviction that enthusiastic modern church worship is tending to nourish this trend. Contrary to all appearances, the trend is in fact towards spiritual shallowness, not depth; and, more often than not, towards social attitudes of *laissez-faire* and conservatism, rather than demands for social change. And because this tendency towards the simplistic, the informal, the 'folksy' and the charismatic has been institutionalized in the infrastructure of worship – with modern hymn books, service books and Bibles – I have no idea what to do about it. Another Cranmer is not the least among the blessings for which England today cries out.

Many of the liturgical changes stem from the decision of the Church of Rome to replace Latin. With the Roman Catholics leaping from mediaeval to modern times in one gigantic stride, the pressure was on for everybody else to follow suit. The results have been mixed. Some are good; but a great deal are not good enough. Again, I record my conviction that with Anglican-Methodist union, it would all have been different.

When the scheme foundered, I was distraught. I had come to believe that under God, I had been equipped to exercise a ministry in the context of a uniting English church. I had a profound feeling for history, and a catholic spirit which embraced Sankeys as sincerely as Gregorian chant. When it became clear that the great event was not going to happen because the church (the Church of England, to be exact) was too cowardly and too obdurately sinful to see how late was the hour, the sense of futility and disillusionment was overwhelming. How to respond? – that was the question. Not to leave God's service – that, at least, was for sure; and to rejoice that the matter was, ultimately, in Divine, not human, hands. But the conviction that God had opened a door and we had slammed it shut was bitter knowledge. Henceforth, I vowed to concentrate on a ministry spent largely 'in the world'. To denominations, as such, I would pay minimal regard, serving where invited, and worshipping where opportunity permitted. To reach the unconverted, and to work to transform the spirit of England – these would remain my priorities. So it has proved, and I have found immense joy in the service of God. But to my dying day, I shall believe that we could have taken this generation by the scruff of the neck, and challenged it meaningfully with the claims of the living God if we had not let Anglican-Methodist unity slip through our fingers. 'Living and working together', setting up joint committees, producing worship which is uniformly bland, and exciting ourselves with pentecostal gestures, are no substitute for the heights and depths, the agonies and the ecstasies of real religion – the religion which becomes immersed in the complexities and compromises of modern society and challenges it with the Word of Life. That's what *might* have been. The present reality is that nobody is taking much notice – and don't let anyone tell you differently. The opportunity was thrown away – not least by so-called 'catholics' who either were scared, or didn't understand the meaning of catholicity. They took their eye off the ball – the mission of the church and the quality of our national life – and played 'denominations'. But Christ isn't interested in that game. Christ is interested in the spirit which resides in our heart; how much love is there, how much compassion, how much vision. If England needs a revival, it is not a revival of Roman Catholicism, or Anglicanism, or any other 'ism'. It is a revival of that reverent, inquiring, catholic spirit, which recognizes that truth has many guises, and that 'piety' without charity is nothing worth. This spirit bestrides all denominational divides, emphasizing and celebrating the things which unite, while ever pressing forward to new and greater truths. Above all, it recognizes that ecclesiastical differences, however interesting to the connoisseur, come second always to the claims of the Kingdom. The quality of our common life, and the message of Divine Love, are ever our first concern. The historic failure of the Anglican-Methodist conversations, and the fateful consequences, will remain a standing rebuke and a perpetual warning.

Without diluting, in any way, the historic uniqueness of the Christian tradition in the life of England, this new, catholic spirit must embrace also the other world faiths now equally indigenous to this land. Enmity and rivalry belong to the past. It is time for mutual respect, warmth, friendship, and humility. Such attitudes clash in no way with a firm faith stoutly maintained. And no Christian should ever let pass an opportunity of commending his master. But the Spirit is all; and, today, the spirit should be that of sharing, and of loving, and of learning humbly from one another. If a second chamber continues to form part of the British parliament, it would be good to see not only Anglican bishops, but also elected representatives of other major British Christian denominations. Also present should be representatives of those other faiths which have long been part of the English religious scene. Natural justice, catholic spirit, and national unity demand it.

England's new revival must embrace, thirdly, an unambigious social dimension. The various churches should not, of course, take out corporate membership of any particular political party! The church is not that kind of organization. Its members, however, should cultivate a much more lively social awareness. The 'love' of which the New Testament speaks is not some kind of spiritual abstract, or a purely personal phenomenon. It is not simply about being kind to one homeless person. It is about attacking and removing homelessness. Love requires policies and programmes to express itself, just as it requires warm hearts and brave spirits. Any revival of religion which did not prompt a new vision of social justice would be a waste of time. It would be counterfeit, and phoney. The love of Jesus, which unites us as children of one Father, constrains and compels us to seek a society in which our brotherhood and sisterhood can find expression. The politics – the ways and means of getting there – are the responsibility of the politicians and those particularly interested in such matters. But the responsibility for supplying the basic principles, and for stating clearly the goals we want to achieve and the kind of society we want to create, rests upon every person, and especially upon those who bow at the name of Jesus. Despite the clouded witness of so many, committed Christian discipleship cannot be separated from an obligation to seek and vote for radical social change. It is in this sense that politics and religion are two sides of the same coin. Until we have seen that 'love' is both personal and social, we have not seen Jesus. It is not a question of choosing one or the other. You are committed to both; or you are committed to neither.

In modern Britain, where Tory governments have dominated, audacious attempts have been made to justify conservative policies by claiming them to be in harmony with Christian teaching. In one widely-reported speech made in September 1993, Michael Portillo asserted that Christians had a moral responsibility to reduce the welfare state and help restore the individual's sense of personal responsibility towards others. Too broad a benefit system undermined the morale of those who received help. He claimed that, for many people, the role of government had sapped their sense of responsibility towards other people. It was hard to be neighbourly if we were told that the state should look after our neighbours.

Mr Portillo admitted that Christian teaching urged us to be generous and to share our wealth with others, but the Christian message was not about taxation, public spending, and collective charity. The call to do good, which lay at the heart of Christianity, demanded an individual response. Good could not be done by proxy or by the state. He argued that there were great moral hazards in allowing the state to become too big. It was hard to be responsible within our families if we were told that the state should educate our children, teach them right and wrong, and for that matter, care for our elderly relatives. We would end up by virtually renouncing any responsibility for the way our society developed, or for its customs and morals.

It is always difficult for the person-in-the-pew to avoid charges of naivety when venturing to comment on the implications of the Christian gospel for the ordering of our common life. Politics, economics, and social issues of every kind are invariably complex. With only a little knowledge, it is easy to say something silly. The temptation, therefore, is to listen to the 'experts', deferring to their greater knowledge and experience, and leave these disturbing and complicated matters in their capable hands . . . At which point naivety becomes gullibility! It is a no-win situation. Say something, and you're wrong; say nothing, and you're even more wrong! However, there is no escaping the dilemma. Here, as in so many aspects of Christian discipleship, we have to do the best we can in the imperfect circumstances which surround us. Using our heads and hearts, we have to try to discern and interpret what the principle of love implies, then try to apply it. When we get it wrong, we have to repent, or apologize, or reconsider – then pick ourselves up, dust ourselves down, and hope we do better next time.

Important words like 'freedom', 'choice', and 'responsibility' easily lose their meaning on the lips of right-wing politicians and become, instead, a deceitful, heartless, and hollow sham. If I am poor and struggling to make ends meet, my hypothetical freedoms are, in practice, severely circumscribed by my economic circumstances. My theoretical choices are purely illusionary, for in reality the cheapest option is the only option. And as for morale and a sapped sense of responsibility, no one wondering where the next pound is coming from (and burdened, perhaps by a crippling council tax bill) gives such luxuries a second thought! Survival becomes the name of the game. Assistance assists, not defiles, and it is when neighbourliness is embodied in the state that it is most effective – and the state itself ennobled. Such statutory provision will always leave room for acts of personal generosity and kindness. To pretend otherwise is transparent nonsense. For that reason, Mr Portillo's words sounded trivial and unconvincing on that occasion, not radiating warmth, but appearing, instead, to betray hardness of heart. Many may agree with him – but that is not to their credit, and doesn't affect my verdict. For Mr Portillo was wrong, I suspect, in most of his reported assertions.

The Christian message – that 'God is love' and that we should 'love one another' – is about the centrality to human life of kindness, tenderness, compassion, self-sacrifice and justice. These are the meaning of love and their claim upon us is equally and indivisibly personal and social, as I have tried already to indicate. In that context, the Christian message – when it is made incarnate, when it is given flesh and form and practical expression – most certainly *is* about taxation, public spending, and 'collective charity', especially if 'charity' is used in its New Testament sense, and not with the derogatory modern overtones it has acquired. (Perhaps I do Mr Portillo wrong, but I can't help suspecting he was employing the latter.) The gospel does, indeed, invite a response from each individual person – and that response is both personal (concerning the kind of person I am, and feel I ought to be), and social (concerning the kind of society and world I would like to inhabit). The second part of the vision of love is pursued not only by trying to convert individuals, but by policies, programmes, and votes. Many people unmoved by dogma and doctrine, and not given to spiritual self-examination, are nonetheless open to lofty visions of a nobler society. They may have to be pushed and cajoled, but it can be done. (The fact that, in Britain, the task has currently been made harder by the appalling success of successive Conservative governments in altering the spiritual values and perceptions of the nation in no way weakens this assertion. On the contrary, it illustrates and confirms it. If people can be made to think and act selfishly and greedily, there must be a hope that they can also be encouraged to act worthily and compassionately.) Good *can* be done by the state, and done to millions who, as individuals, we shall never meet. Good *can* be done by proxy – a silly, loaded phrase, but since it was employed it must be seized and turned on the user. Why should 'good' cease to be good when it proceeds from an authorized person or agent? If legislators of only average moral merit (when viewed as individuals) can nevertheless be persuaded to pass good laws, many people will benefit – just as many suffer when evil or unjust laws are effected. Whatever we mean by 'good' and 'evil', the fundamental truth is this: that they reside not only in individuals, but in systems. And systems can be improved, to the great benefit of the poorest and weakest, without waiting for people like Mr Portillo and me to achieve sainthood! (Even that unlikely eventuality would not affect many, without policies and laws to embody the love in our hearts.)

Of course, welfare provision is abused! Every good thing is abused and all reasonable care should be taken to contain it. But to use that abuse by a minority as an excuse for reducing welfare provision for the most vulnerable members of our society is despicable; and to assert that benefits undermine the morale of recipients is humbug. When powerful men seize on trivial matters to inflame public prejudice (unmindful of how puny and laughable they look) it is time to take guard. Remember the foreign social security scroungers . . . and the young offenders taken on exotic foreign holidays . . . ? When right wing politicians claim to be speaking with the authority of the New Testament, it is time for more than raised eyebrows. It is time to protest. England's revival must see us as one nation, united in a sense of comradeship, care, and true responsibility for one another. Such attitudes will not find their expression in the policies associated with Mr Portillo's wing of the political spectrum.

However, some would disagree, preferring to side with Mr Portillo. Fundamentalism and pentecostalism on the one hand, and the Pope's reactionary conservatism on the other, have helped to generate attitudes of sternness and authoritarianism in the face of the nation's perceived weakness and godlessness. Such people might well be attracted by the title of this book – before throwing it down in horror! – because 'revival' is a theme dear to their hearts. Pity poor England should such a 'revival' occur: an outbreak of religious enthusiasm allied to right-wing political extremism. It would represent a horrifying lurch towards fascism.

Anyone tempted to regard such reflections as unrealistic and alarmist should understand that there are elements in Christian tradition, both Catholic and Protestant, which are open and vulnerable to fascist development. Conversely, there are elements in fascism which have a particular appeal to religious people. Kenneth Leech gave a frightening list of these in an article which appeared in *The Guardian* of 26 June 1993, 'Fascist cancer in the heartland of Christianity'. They include the belief in total certainty and total control; a contempt for the mind, and insistence on uncritical acceptance of authority from above; the belief that the world is decaying and must be rescued from nihilism and rootlessness; the emphasis on tradition, inequality, stern laws, and warfare against decadence; the appeal to the heroic; nationalism and patriotism; and the appeal of security and stability in exchange for freedom and justice.

A revival of religion which opened the door to an upsurge of fascism would be a curse, not a blessing. England needs a revival, but a revival that radiates the gentleness and compassion of the gospel, and finds its political expression in policies which pursue justice and the things which belong to our peace.

The attitudes which have dominated the British political scene over recent years have created a feeling that survival in a hostile world is possible only by people's own individual efforts. This, in turn, engenders an attitude which encourages ruthlessness, greed, selfishness, and the exploitation of the weak and vulnerable. Without minimizing the importance of personal responsibility, there are other emphases Christians should also want to stress, and which concern our responsibilities towards one another. Not all of us are capable of defending and providing for ourselves in every respect. The very young, the old, the weak and frail, the disabled, the sick, the poor and those on low incomes – the list is a long one. A renewal of Christianity would involve more than well-dressed and well-heeled people continuing to keep the roof on their local church, admirable as that may be. It would involve widespread support for policies intended to even out many of our inequalities and to generate a new, civilizing awareness that our lives are bound up together. A revival which produced anything less would be, at best, irrelevant and phoney. We belong to one another! High or low, we can enrich each other's lives if we get our act together, and plan and act as one family! A revival of that spirit would transform our land.

The revival for which England cries out must include a strong and central element of concern for the environment. Here, at least, there are embers of hope waiting to be fanned to a flame. Today, young people have become increasingly sensitive to the importance of environmental issues. I regard that sensitivity as virtually a religious impulse in its own right – not merely an urgent expression of the survival instinct, but rather a profound and intuitive awareness of our relationship to the planet. Men, women and earth form one organic whole. Given this awareness, any religious revival which failed to respond to and embrace such an awakening would be worse than worthless. Heaven is our Christian hope, and provides the glorious perspective from which we view all human endeavour. But God created heaven and earth; the Word was made flesh; and – for the moment – the earth is our home, and our Mother.

Photographs of our planet, taken from space, are extraordinarily beautiful and uniquely moving. Yet the most casual reflection should alert us to the fact that something is seriously wrong. When I was a boy, outings to the seaside were a rare treat. How we revelled in the joyful combination of sunshine, water and fresh air! The story is not quite the same today. We still flock to the beaches but – if we have any sense – a wariness accompanies us. Too much exposure to strong sunlight has become positively dangerous; the sea is often contaminated with sewage and threatens disease; and the wind carries impure air to quiet and beautiful places many miles from the source of the pollution, causing and aggravating respiratory problems in environments where people had imagined themselves least at risk.

It has been apparent for many years that Britain's countryside is dying, with once-common plants disappearing, and features such as hedgerows, ponds and walls, which sheltered wildlife, being destroyed. A recent Department of the Environment survey showed that over the previous decade, most of Britain had suffered a severe reduction in the diversity of plants. One of the most disturbing features was that traditional 'sanctuaries' of wild plants – hedgerows, river banks, and roadside verges – had suffered a loss in diversity even when not physically damaged by agricultural or other disturbance.

By now, everybody knows that acid rain is killing our trees. From time to time, new disasters alarm us, like the red-leg disease which is presently threatening our frogs. Modern industry, our technological skill and the demands of a rapidly-increasing human population have subjected the planet to what might with justification be best described as acute stress. With a dramatic suddenness, occupying little more that the flicker of an eye-lid in geological time, the forests have shrunk by half, atmospheric carbon dioxide levels have soared and the ozone layer of the stratosphere has thinned and holes have opened at the poles. The population of the human species has doubled over the past fifty years. No other species (to quote Professor Edward O. Wilson of Harvard University) has remotely approached the sheer mass in protoplasm generated by humanity.

All these facts are familiar, which is the reason I merely refer to them rather than discuss them at length. The important point is that it is not too late – yet – to address these issues and in large measure to retrieve the situation (though the extinction of species is now proceeding at a horrifying rate). There are sound reasons for optimism. Some of the damage can be restored, and the conservation of biodiversity is being recognized as crucial to the well-being of the planet and to the human race. We do not as a species exist in isolation, but as an integral part of complex, inter-related ecosystems. Professor Wilson again:

> Each species occupies a niche, demanding a certain place, an exact microclimate, particular nutrients, and temperature and humidity cycles with specified timing to trigger phases of the life cycle. Many, perhaps most, of the species are locked in symbioses with other species; they cannot survive and reproduce unless arrayed with their partners in the correct configurations.

Throughout the world religion is becoming increasingly 'green', with its leaders recognizing environmental problems as moral issues. A revival of religion in England could only reinforce that process. Failure to do so would be denial of the God who saw everything that he had made and, behold, it was very good.

The religious revival our country needs must, fifthly, evince a mature attitude to human sexuality. How easy to say! Alas, a gloom, a heaviness and a sense of futility descend after only a moment's reflection on the track record of Christians, on this most crucial of all themes. Put bluntly, we tend usually to be unrealistic and hypocritical. Often we are liars. We display little evidence of having thought about the subject with brave and simple honesty before mouthing our platitudes. As a result, our views are not taken seriously. One wonders how seriously we take them ourselves.

Elementary facts of life cause us extraordinary difficulty. We find it easier, by far, to recite traditional responses than to wrestle and think things through for ourselves. The inability of some Christian people to recognize and admit the living power of human sexuality – its undeniability and its need to find expression – reduces many of their arguments to the point of absurdity. This is particularly evident, for example, when the sexuality of the unmarried is under discussion. If masturbation, prostitution, and fornication are all ruled out, vivid nocturnal fantasies seem all that is on offer. Yet Christians have traditionally prayed to be delivered from 'evil' thoughts and 'phantoms of the night', so (although the prayer asks for an impossibility), even that lonely form of release is denied. Dreams are out!

Our dishonest and ill-informed attitudes to homosexuality provide perhaps the clearest modern illustration of our inability or unwillingness to think beyond our prejudices (and our selected biblical texts). Our record of hypocrisy, persecution and purblindness in this matter has turned the question of a person's attitude to gay rights into a remarkably accurate touchstone. It is a sure and sensitive indicator of realistic, informed and compassionate discipleship. To dismiss automatically as shameful something capable of being tender, wholesome and good is an unworthy response for a follower of Jesus. One of the unloveliest sights in the world is to watch Christian people, fulfilled within the security of a happy marriage, meting out judgment upon others who have not been so lucky. A few lonely nights in an empty bed would, perchance, work wonders, both for their imagination and for their charity.

The Roman Catholic Church faces special problems at the present time. These difficulties are of its own making and relate to teachings which undoubtedly will be reversed in years to come. However, in the meantime it has attracted the near disbelief and contempt of a vast number of ordinary people. Its attitudes to contraception, masturbation, homosexuality and clerical celibacy have laid insupportable burdens on the shoulders of its own people, and made itself an object of derision in the eyes of others. Of course, reflections like these sound out of place in this ecumenical age, but they are made in love, and with sadness mingled with the despair. But when a great church has come near to institutionalizing hypocrisy – as it assuredly has over contraception and clerical celibacy – its friends have a duty to protest. These days, we sink or swim together. The duplicity and double standards apply not only in the lower ranks. Listening sometimes to leaders in positions of authority – who, on virtually any other subject are heard with respect – it is occasionally impossible to decide whether they themselves are deceived, disingenous or deceitful. Until the Roman church can bring itself to address matters relating to human sexuality in the manner of people who live in the same world as the rest of us, many of the important things they have to say on a range of vital matters will fall largely on stony ground. Their credibility problem is as serious as that.

Few Christians, however, seem truly at ease when sexual themes are under discussion. No topics are more central to our lives – as individuals or as a community – but our insights seem so limited. Throughout the debates on the ordination of women, I waited eagerly for evidence of fresh creative thinking on the subject of the relationship between men and women. There was irrefutable evidence of misogyny, but little which suggested a sensitive awareness of the subleties of human sexuality. Perhaps we've nothing to say on the subject. If that's the case, the least we can do is not to muddy the waters for those who have.

Perhaps novelists, poets and writers are better placed to

explore these matters. Free from any obligation to conform to traditional dogmas, and free to explore important and interesting themes, their work complements that of the philosopher and theologian, and often exceeds it in clarity of perception and power of impact.

Since the trial of *Lady Chatterley's Lover*, which drew my student attention to the work of a writer of whom previously I had never heard, I have turned for inspiration again and again to the work of D. H. Lawrence. Here are a few brief examples, concerning the permanence of marriage, the relationship between man and woman, and the relationship between man and man

Nobody writes about marriage more wisely and movingly than D. H. Lawrence. Take these words from his essay 'A Propos of Lady Chatterley's Lover':

> Is not a man different, utterly different, at dawn from what he is at sunset? And a woman too? And does not the changing harmony and discord of their variation make the secret music of life?

> And is it not so throughout life? A man is different at thirty, at forty, at fifty, at sixty, at seventy: and the woman at his side is different. But is there not some strange conjunction in their differences? . . . is there not, throughout it all, some unseen, unknown interplay of balance, harmony, completion, like some soundless symphony, made out of the soundless singing of two strange and incompatible lives, a man's and a woman's . . .

> Mankind has got to get back to the rhythm of the cosmos, and the permanence of marriage.

In *Women in Love* he wrote on the relationship between men and women with beauty and simplicity:

> 'What I want is a strange conjunction with you -' he said quietly; '- not meeting and mingling . . . but an equilibrium, a pure balance of two single beings: - as the stars balance each other.'

'I did not say, nor imply, a satellite. I meant two single stars
balanced in conjunction –'

On the ties of attraction and repulsion which exist between
men – which all men feel, yet few dare admit into the
consciousness – he ventured in the same novel with strange
authority where few churchmen dare follow:

They parted with apparent unconcern, as if their going apart
were a trivial occurrence . . . Yet the heart of each burned
for the other . . . This they would never admit. They
intended to keep their relationship a casual free-and-easy
friendship, they were not going to be so unmanly and
unnatural as to allow any heart-burning between them. They
had not the faintest belief in deep relationship between men
and men, and their disbelief prevented any development of
their powerful but suppressed friendliness.

Modern Christians should not be fearful of reverent and
honest reflection when human sexuality is under discussion.
This does not mean that, unthinkingly, we discard traditional
attitudes; still less that we vote for 'anything goes'. But knee-
jerk reactions accompanied by texts are not only counter-
productive; often, they bring harm to ourselves by reinforcing
our personal dishonesty, and encouraging us to sin against the
spirit of truth. Truth is of God, be it revealed by scientist,
novelist or preacher; but it is often the first casualty when
religious people speak of sex.

England, then needs a revival; but not any old revival. To be
a priceless and positive asset to the nation, life-enhancing and
effective, it cannot be based upon fundamentalist attitudes to
scripture; it must be ecumenically-minded and catholic-
spirited; it must embrace the struggle for social justice; it must
be alive to the religious nature of environmental issues; and
it must be capable of helping people to develop informed
and grown-up attitudes to sexual issues. It is a big 'but'. Yet if
by some miracle these things could be, how England would be
glad!

8

Revival and The Holy Trinity

What England needs, and what England will get, are not necessarily the same thing! That our country would benefit from a flowering of the spirit of true religion – humility, wonder, compassion, and tenderness – is manifestly self-evident. But can it be made to happen? And if so, how?

Godly men and women have yearned, for many years, to see a revival of religion in this land. Notable among these saints was Dr W. E. Sangster, the Methodist leader whose name still holds a special fragrance for those whose lives were touched by his ministry, and for whom the sadness of his early death in 1960 has never dimmed. His life was increasingly dominated by a deep and fervent concern for the spiritual health of the nation, and by a longing to witness a revival of religion. Browsing through the reports nearly forty years later, it is still possible to sense the power and the passion of his address to the 1958 Methodist Conference.

> A study of the history of revival shows that when it appears to be sudden, it isn't. There are certain necessary prerequisites for what appears to be a sudden descent of the Holy Ghost. There must be mighty faith and pleading prayer on the part of God's people . . . The text we seek to impress upon our people is that ancient word God said to us concerning the descent of the Holy Spirit to bring revival: 'If My people who are called by My Name shall humble themselves and pray and seek My face and turn from their wicked ways, then will I hear in heaven and heal their sin and redeem their land.'

Dr Sangster proceeded to outline a three-point strategy.

Firstly, it was intended to publish two paper-backed books to give churchgoers a new apologetics, to help them in their own thinking and in their personal acts of evangelism. Secondly, more attention would be given to 'pre-evangelism'. If a man did not believe in the existence of God, or did not know who Jesus Christ was, or if the mention of the Holy Spirit suggested spooks to him, that man was not the subject for evangelism at all. It would be almost wrong to subject him to it. What was needed was pre-evangelism. Thirdly, they had to aim to recover among Christian people that pleading prayer without which nothing would happen. Revival could come without new leaders, it could come without new song, though normally there would be both; but it could not come without prayer.

It is difficult to read his words without being moved, without marvelling at how greatly the world has changed since they were spoken, and without being impressed by the direction in which Dr Sangster was looking. The need to equip Christians to give a reason for the faith that is in them, and the recognition of the importance of 'pre-evangelism', were clear pointers to the future, and link our England of the '90s to that of the '50s. Today intellectual integrity is crucial as never before – which is why the swing towards fundamentalism and pentecostalism is giving religion a bad name, and making us a laughing stock. And a large amount of the work undertaken by the modern church is undoubtedly *pre*-evangelism: preparing ground, removing misunderstanding, building bridges, learning the language, simply being there and waiting for those rare and precious opportunities to communicate a sense of the presence of God, to name the Name, or point to Jesus.

However, despite our endeavours over the intervening years, no revival of religion has taken place, certainly not as envisaged and longed for by Dr Sangster; neither has the soul of the nation been healed. Rather, the symptoms of malady and decay have – among all the small, bright welcome signs of hope – become more pronounced. We face a situation more testing in some ways than that addressed by Dr Sangster forty years ago. Perhaps our expectations have been lowered by the knocks of experience! Our language is different, and our surroundings have altered. Yet the conviction remains that – however it might find worthy expression – the religious impulse of worship, wonder, reverence and awe, together with a spirit of kindness and a thirst for justice, would transform the life of this nation. Setting aside for the moment my conviction that in rejecting the Anglican-Methodist unity conversations, we spurned the most precious practical opportunity my generation is likely to see to influence England for good, what fresh suggestions have we to put alongside those set out by Dr Sangster in 1958, and still so pertinent?

One consideration towers above all others, though I fear it will attract much ridicule. Those charged with leadership in every branch of the holy catholic church in this land must rediscover the centrality to Christian faith and discipleship of the doctrine of the Holy Trinity. While this assertion is unlikely to be greeted with rapturous acclaim, it is nonetheless true.

The nineteenth-century authoress Harriet Martineau made a humorous reference in her autobiography to Thomas Madge, one of the ministers of the famous Octagon Chapel in Norwich, which stands a few yards from my front door. 'One evening when I was a child, I entered the parlour when our Unitarian minister, Mr Madge, was convicting of error (and what he called idiotcy) an orthodox schoolmaster who happened to be our visitor. "Look here," said Mr Madge, seizing three wine glasses, and placing them in a row. "Here is the Father, here's the Son, – and here's the Holy Ghost; do you mean to tell me that these three glasses can be in any case one? 'Tis mere nonsense."' (The house in which the incident occurred is today my doctors' surgery).

It is still easy for clever unbelievers to have fun at our expense in this vein, but that should not perturb us. On the contrary, if we lose sight of the doctrine of the Holy and Undivided Trinity, and see it as anything other than the supreme theological expression of the mystery, majesty, and holiness of God, we're done for. Yet the danger is real. When I read that a prominent bishop had suggested that the church should be re-named 'The Jesus Movement', I frowned very deeply. Before I'd had time to recover, an article on multi-faith Britain appeared in the religious column of a national newspaper, expounding the notion that closer understanding could be achieved if each religion was willing to consider setting aside some of its more obscure or contentious doctrines. Instantly, I was wary, and on guard – yet I was still more than a little taken aback when the doctrine of the Holy Trinity was nominated as the Christian contribution to this process. Unimpressed, I waited with no small anticipation for the indignant response. To my surprise, it never came. If letters were written, they were not published, and I was left disappointed and uneasy. I was not taught to regard the mystery of the Holy and Undivided Trinity as an optional extra. In my experience, authentic catholic Christian discipleship is inevitably and always an expression of Trinitarian faith.

In one of his most popular books, another famous Methodist preacher, Dr Leslie Weatherhead, imagined St Peter being instructed in the Christian faith as summarized in the Athanasian creed, one of the bed-rock documents of the church. You may remember how, at one point, it declares:

The Father uncreate, the Son uncreate, and the Holy Ghost uncreate.
The Father incomprehensible, the Son incomprehensible, and the Holy Ghost incomprehensible.
The Father eternal, the Son eternal, and the Holy Ghost eternal.
And yet they are not three eternals, but one eternal.
As also there are not three incomprehensibles, nor three uncreated, but one uncreated, and one incomprehensible.

It continues in the same vein for what seems to be page after page until this gem is reached:

This is the Catholick Faith: which except a man believe faithfully, he cannot be saved.

Dr Weatherhead observed drily that long before that point had been reached, St Peter would have interrupted: 'I go a- fishing!' – adding: 'And I would go with him.'

The doctrine of the Holy Trinity is not the starting-point for the evangelist. I hope nobody suggests otherwise. But neither is it the dead-weight implied in the tale of the old rural rascal who went to church only on Trinity Sunday, 'To hear the parson tie himself up in knots!'

There is, however, a mysterious wholeness in the teaching of Christ, and in the faith of the church, which constitutes the heart of Christian discipleship and without which it becomes rapidly enfeebled and misshapen. Put bluntly, mature Christian discipleship should be an expression and reflection of the Holy Trinity.

I glory in the doctrine! I exult in its grandeur, and hide in its unfathomable vastness. Isaac Watts' great Trinitarian hymn, 'We give immortal praise', concludes:

> Almighty God, to Thee
>   Be endless honours done,
> The undivided Three,
>   And the mysterious One.
> Where reason fails, with all her powers,
> There faith prevails and love adores.

And therein lies the doctrine's fundamental and everlasting value! It prevents us from capturing God, of mastering one important insight into the mystery and imagining that a fragmentary part is the inexpressible whole. The doctrine of the Holy Trinity is not a deliberate affront to reason, but a reminder of reason's limitations. It is the church's formal acknowledgment that the themes with which we toy, and the eternal issues in which we attempt to dabble, are vast beyond our comprehension. They can never be solved or subdued – ever teasing and beckoning, yet ever eluding our grasp. But it was not concocted for that purpose! It was never merely a useful but temporary device which, sooner or later, could be safely jettisoned. The Holy Trinity represents the heart of the Christian revelation, and its celebration is the crown of the Christian year! The doctrine was not the product of philosophers. It was the product of experience.

This is manifestly not a weighty study in systematic theology
– would that I were so capable! These are the reflections of an
ineffective twentieth-century evangelist who – in an age of
disbelief, and burdened with the conviction that the failure of
the Anglican-Methodist unity proposals was a calamity never to
be undone – claims only to have tried. Clumsy, feeble,
underwritten by too little study and prayer – all these charges
and worse are true. But I've tried – tried to ignore denominations; tried to break out of the ghetto-mentality to which
churchmen easily succumb (regarding religion as an end,
whereas life is the end, and religion a tool); tried to maintain a
high Christian profile in a society where religion counts for
little. I hope I've comforted a few, supported and encouraged a
few, and stimulated a few – but I've not won new members. *But
I've tried* – and the driving force, the constant, fixed assumption, and the relentless inspiration of my Christian discipleship
and my ministry has been the doctrine of the Holy and
Undivided Trinity.

Please excuse my linguistic shorthand and my theological
shortcomings in these reflections. I believe devoutly that the
Holy Trinity is involved in every Divine action. Overlook my
crudeness if I appear to confound the Persons or divide the
Substance – to quote Athanasius again.

The Father we associate with the divine majesty and divine
splendour, never more gloriously evoked than in the incompar-
able sixth chapter of Isaiah:

I saw . . . the Lord sitting upon a throne, high and lifted up,
and his train filled the temple. Above it stood the seraphims:
each one had six wings; with twain he covered his face, and
with twain he covered his feet, and with twain he did fly. And
one cried unto another, and said, Holy, holy, holy, is the
Lord of hosts: the whole earth is full of his glory. And the
posts of the door moved at the voice of him that cried, and the
house was filled with smoke . . .

Let Stainer's setting of those noble words permeate into the
distant recesses of your mind and being, and Trinity Sunday

will never be the same again. 'This, this is the God we adore'. It can never be emphasized too strongly or too frequently that discipleship has its roots in this dimension of awe, reverence, wonder, mystery, fear, and majesty. 'Thou great, mysterious God unknown,' sang Wesley, in a paradoxical yet memorable phrase which sets all our wonderings in their only possible realistic context: majesty and immensity, 'beyond all knowledge and all thought'.

Any discipleship worth the name contains an element of holy fear and of humility before the mystery, an awareness of the Father's immensity and unmanageability. This attitude of quiet reverence runs through the gospel portrayal of Jesus, from 'Consider the lilies of the field' to his love of synagogue and temple. What practical effect should this have on us, who profess to be his followers? It should not make us joyless, pompous, proud, or full of airs and graces, that's for sure! But there should be a hint of eternity in the bearing of a Christian, a kind of dignity; an awareness that we are dealing in unfathomable and holy things. If this is lacking, our discipleship is holed below the water-line, and becomes fatally distorted. Whatever we are attempting for God becomes quickly unconvincing and sounds hollow and trite. For those called to conduct worship, this has particular relevance (as I have implied already). Undue familiarity induces a sense of unreality in public worship. Even our most tender expressions of devotion should preserve the distinction between Creator and creature, clearly and unambiguously. 'Tremble, O earth, at the presence of the Lord; at the presence of the God of Israel.' That – in part, and with childish simplicity – is the contribution of the Father to Christian discipleship.

The Son we associate with the tenderness, compassion, and self-sacrificial love displayed by our Lord Jesus Christ. How it revolutionized the lives of those it touched! 'The half of my goods I give to the poor,' vowed Zaccheus, after the encounter that turned his world upside-down. 'Come and see a man which told me all things that ever I did,' exclaimed the woman at the well after being brought face-to-face with the stark realities of her moral and spiritual condition. Meeting Jesus meant that, whatever paths she chose, her world had changed for ever. A veil had been drawn aside. That discussion about living water would remain vivid in her memory.

Many who met Jesus were healed in body as a result. We can only wonder at the precise nature of those healing processes. Christ's teaching and his very presence imparted a kind of positive energy which exorcised the negative influences – like guilt, vengeance, hatred, and the feeling of being unloved – which unquestionably undermine our physical health. But the 'mechanics' are in a sense unimportant. The fact is that the name of Jesus was and remains synonymous with healing. Others, no less wonderfully, were healed in mind and spirit. In Lloyd Douglas' novel *The Robe*, a most beautiful portrait is drawn of a girl called Miriam. She is lame, and we meet her first in the market place, in the evening, where she is carried on a frame each day by her friends. There, as the sun sets, she sings the psalms and other ancient songs of her people, in a voice of such beauty and richness that all who listen are deeply affected. We discover, however, that she had not always sung. On the contrary, she had been a girl consumed with bitterness, and resentful at the injustice of her affliction. One day, Jesus had passed that way, and had visited and talked with her. The details of their conversation she never disclosed, but the consequences could not be hidden! Her entire demeanour was affected. She smiled; she became wise and understanding. Above all, she discovered she could sing . . . 'He hath put a new song in my mouth . . . ' Her voice brought consolation and inspiration to her neighbours. She remained lame, but in mind and spirit she had been made whole: a 'miracle' equally wondrous and exciting. No words exist to convey what it must have meant to look into the eyes of Jesus. Some found hope and strength beyond their wildest dreams. Others, like Peter and Judas, found self-knowledge that drove them to the very edge of despair, and beyond.

Christian discipleship means falling under the spell of the Divine Love. We bear Christ's name, and have no theoretical difficulty in setting the Son at the centre of our religious lives. Yet the word 'Christian' means nothing very vital or meaningful unless it signifies commitment to Christ's way of love, and to his living Spirit.

This commitment – I need scarcely reiterate – is personal. How our discipleship comes under the spotlight at this point. 'Gentle Jesus, meek and mild' must be the most misunderstood line in English hymnody, derided because words change their meaning, and our age has grown ever more shallow. But Jesus was gentle – see him with the children, with women, with sinners, with his friends; and neither meekness nor mildness are marks of weakness but of strength held perfectly in great control. Gentle, strong, calm, just and kind – Jesus was all these things, and more. There was an indefinable quality about him, as if his ultimate allegiance was to another kingdom, where different values and criteria applied . . . And that, too, should be the bearing of a follower of Jesus. Discipleship excludes constant agitation over status, wealth and influence. Instead, it rejoices in the supreme Christian paradox – the secret which we ourselves find so hard to believe – that our very vulnerability and helplessness, when combined with a spirit of love, is the source of our greatest influence.

Commitment to the way of love is, equally, social. I find it necessary to emphasize this truth repeatedly. Jesus mixed effortlessly with all types of people, but was known not as the friend of the rich merchants, but as the friend of publicans and sinners. Both the Lord's Prayer and the Sermon on the Mount are weighted heavily in favour of the poor, while the reason why we do not choke on the Magnificat escapes me. Our witness is not good. The church makes brave and well-informed statements, though they are not always as good as they ought to be (gay rights providing the classic example), but too many individual Christians keep their heads down. We become as aquisitive and status-orientated as everybody else, and vote unhesitatingly for politicians who pursue policies which favour the rich. One suspects that, in truth, we too would have found an itinerant carpenter with a few fishermen friends talking about love and about a kingdom in which traditional values were stood on their heads a great trial.

Loyalty to Jesus, the divine Son, means taking his teaching seriously – not merely the letter, but the clear, underlying spirit. It means commitment to a love inescapably personal and social: not merely one or the other, but both. That – in part, and with even greater simplicity – is the contribution of the Son to Christian discipleship.

The Holy Ghost, for so long the missing person of the Trinity, has in this generation regained a rightful place in the church's thinking and (in theory, at least) in the life of the Christian disciple. The Father's awful holiness, immensity and mystery can contribute to a sense of Divine remoteness. The green hill far away, where the Son suffered and died can – at two thousand years and two thousand miles – seem too far away. But the Holy Spirit is God our contemporary, God in the present, God in action (to use Bishop Cockin's inspired phrase). The Holy Spirit brings freshness to our discipleship with the expectation that God will act *now*. Without this hope that the God who was – and is – active in creation, who 'spake by the prophets' and spoke uniquely through the Son, will speak to *our* hearts and be active in our world today, there will be no spark of faith to fan into the flame of revival. But God is not imprisoned on a distant star, nor locked away securely in the pages of history. Christians look for signs of God's presence, day by day.

It is possible to know a great deal about the scriptures, and the church, and the life of Christ, yet remain untouched, unaffected, uninvolved and unconverted. It can all be static and academic unless the Holy Spirit makes it dynamic and experiential. Yet a word of caution is necessary again, one which may disappoint but hardly surprise those who have been pained already by my attitudes to fundamentalism and pentecostalism. The Holy Spirit has become equated recently with phenomena such as speaking with tongues and other features of so-called charismatic renewal. This type of religion I find, personally, totally unhelpful. There is clearly nothing exclusively Christian about it, being a phenomenon exhibited by frenzied ecstatics and dervishes of various religions in every age. The Christian doctrine of the Holy Spirit has more substance than this. For those who long for revival, the work of the Holy Ghost is crucial. For those who do not understand, let me spell out the work of the Spirit.

The Holy Spirit gives the *vision*, the sanctified imagination, which points us to Christ, and makes real for us today the pictures, painted by Jesus, of what we and our world could and should be like. The Holy Spirit gives the *will*, the desire that these things should happen in us, and in our world. The Holy Spirit gives the *power*, the Divine energy which we are offered, capable of changing our nature radically and fundamentally, turning Christ the example into Christ the Saviour. The Holy Spirit gives the *wisdom*, helps us to interpret the scriptures and to make right judgments. That, in part, is the contribution of the Holy Spirit to Christian discipleship.

Father, Son and Holy Ghost – each is involved intimately in the adventure to which God invites us. It is not the church; it is not the Bible; it is not any other Christian insight you may care to nominate – it is the doctrine of the Holy and Undivided Trinity which supplies the balance and comprehensiveness which intensifies our discipleship and invests it with authority. A direct connection exists between these elementary thoughts on Christian discipleship and the mission of the church to the people of this land.

Firstly, that essential balance – that wholeness, roundness, fullness and true catholicity – is not always evident in the church's witness today. Although the parallel is not exact, I am reminded again of D. H. Lawrence's response to the various reactions prompted by one of his novels. He declared that between the narrow-minded, who were shocked and uttered condemnation; and the bright young things who did just as they liked, and thought the book a fuss about nothing; and the low, uncultured person with a dirty mind, 'this book has hardly a space to turn in'. Lawrence concluded: 'I stick to my book and my position: Life is only bearable when the mind and the body are in harmony, and there is a natural balance between them.'

Sometimes, I feel that between those who over-emphasize the importance of ritual and continuity and those who over-emphasize the importance of being 'saved', and those who make the church sound like an arm of the DSS and those who can play no record other than their version of the gifts of the Holy Spirit, Trinitarian catholic Christianity 'has hardly a space to turn in'! To parody Lawrence: I stick to my position. The faith of the Christian church is only tenable when the harmony between the Persons of the Holy Trinity is acknowledged, and our discipleship reflects the divine balance between them.

It is possible to find Christians who are keen on social witness, but not so concerned about personal holiness; and Christians with a lively personal faith but who seem unmindful of the terrible majesty of Almighty God; and Christians who display the utmost reverence in their worship but have never been seized with a radical social impulse in their lives. It will not do! This putting asunder of what God has joined together undermines the gospel.

Secondly, what I have called 'the balance' is the fundamental ingredient of our message, and it is vital that we think through, carefully, what it is we are endeavouring to communicate. If our understanding and experience of the faith is not essentially Trinitarian, our discipleship is lopsided, and our witness becomes distorted. Then the revival of religion which England needs retreats still further over the horizon. People seeking to make sense of the various glimpses of God in their lives – which come to us all, though often without religious labels attached – will look elsewhere for meaning, and maybe never find it. The level of blessedness, the amount of life, love, and fulfilment in God's world, will drop a little lower.

A sense of the divine immensity; meekness and warmth in personal relationships and courage and compassion in social attitudes; a longing for the Living God to confront us in our thoughts and in our choices – the challenge is not to perm two out of three (or three out of four). Each of these facets has to be present and evident if our discipleship, however humble, is to have a cutting edge in this remarkable age in which God has called us to serve. Until we are true to our own insights, we shall labour in vain.

9

Dreams of Revival

When we speak of a revival of religion, what is the picture we have in mind? Do we imagine every church and chapel in the land packed to overflowing each Sunday? How exciting that would be, if the religion involved was pure and Christ-like! The qualification is important, for religious mass movements can be dark and sinister, and merely to invoke the name of Jesus does not make them all brightness and light. But however much we might like to imagine tickets for next Sunday's service changing hands at highly-inflated prices, in our bones we suspect that it isn't going to happen. There's no harm in hoping! Nobody knows what the Spirit of God will choose to do next. He blows like a rushing, mighty wind through all our affairs, seemingly at random, ever unpredictable, but fired constantly by Divine Wisdom and Divine Love. Perhaps, as I have been told, it is those of little faith – like me – who are actually standing in the way of the very thing we would love to see! Religion is full of such paradoxes. Indeed, anyone incapable of living with a paradox should avoid religion altogether, particularly Christianity, for the incarnation represents the ultimate in paradox. As Charles Wesley put it:

> Our God contracted to a span,
> Incomprehensibly made man.

I would love to see an outburst of recognizably Christian fervour sweeping the country and manifesting itself in packed churches everywhere. When the word 'revive' occurs in prayers and hymns, I utter it with zeal and hopefulness. But I see no evidence. Neither, I must confess, am I particularly concerned.

The testimony of the Old Testament, the New Testament, and church history suggests strongly that the concept of the faithful 'remnant' has a fundamental place in the divine strategy. God is at work in the life and the institutions of all nations and communities, particularly wherever brave and honest men and women seek truth and justice. No religious structure can confine the living God. But time and again, God has been content, for his special tasks, to use as his instruments despised minorities, small groups, the 'faithful few'. His love for every creature is infinite; but those who love him in return know a tenderness that passeth knowledge. That experience or conviction makes them especially valuable servants of God. This distinction is not rigid. Numbers ebb and flow, and the same God is at work within the church and without, unaffected, as ever, by these and all other divisions and barriers. But the distinction is crucial if we are to prevent the word 'revival' from sinking even lower into the murky underworld of religious jargon and clap-trap. A revival is a quickening: the breathing of new life and energy into a body grown weary or lethargic, or worse! The revival for which England cries out should, realistically and practically, be seen to embrace two distinct, though completely interwoven aspects: the revival of the church and the revival of the nation. These ideas form another paradox: they are separate concepts, yet part of the same divine mission.

If a revival swept through the life of the English churches, attendance at worship and the numbers of those participating in religious activities would undoubtedly swell. There are always a large number of people on the fringe of church activities. They have excuses, reasons and other commitments, all of which keep them from participating fully in the life of the church. The real explanations, of course, lie usually just below the surface. For instance, the churchgoing habit, if it ever existed, has been lost. Churchgoing is not socially unacceptable, but it is unusual enough to be noticed and commented upon. However, if the churches were to recapture that quality of devotion and genuine religious vitality which makes the Book of Acts a beacon for all time, not only would the waverers and sympathizers on the fringe be drawn in, the impact would be much more profound. Even those who at present never give a moment's thought to church membership (happy to see others doing so, but themselves preferring politics or the pub or a football match) would sit up and take notice if the churches were hit with an intense and powerful renewal of their inner life.

Although we live in an age of rationalism, materialism, doubt and disbelief, Christianity would become incomparably more credible and challenging if it was more obviously 'delivering the goods'. If the hallmark of its members was, in truth, a spirit of love . . . If the sacred scriptures were revered and opened eagerly, yet bibliolatry shunned as a deadly sin . . . If each eucharistic feast took us back, in spirit, to Calvary and forward, in spirit to glory . . . If we viewed human sexuality as evidence of God's goodness, and were tender to those whose orientation differed from our own . . . If we were fearless of truth (even when scientific research produced unexpected results) recognizing that all truth is truth about God . . . If we were noted for the simplicity of our life-styles and our love for the planet . . . If our hearts were free and our commitment to social justice as innocent and self-evident as that of Archbishop Desmond Tutu . . . If we refused to take ourselves too seriously . . . If the power in our prayers could be sensed . . . If our churches were enfolded in a sense of the numinous . . . If our singing expressed our joy . . . If our silences spoke of eternity . . . the church would grow! Such spiritual authority would not only be welcomed eagerly; it would, to many people, be almost irresistible!

Those are some of the marks I would expect a revived church to display. I would no longer expect to see endless financial crises; but I *would* expect to see changed lives. I would expect to see men and women healed in body, mind and spirit, as harmony was restored between themselves and their Maker and Saviour. A revived church, therefore, would almost certainly be a larger church – which would do England nothing but good. But infinitely more important than numbers is quality: and here comes the paradox again. I want the earth to be filled with the glory of God as the waters cover the sea. I believe the issues at stake when Jesus was crucified affected every human person. The gospel invitation is to all. But I am drawn back repeatedly to the remnant: to the fact that however large our congregations grow, it seems exceedingly likely that we shall always remain a minority, the salt which gives the savour, the leaven in the lump of God's creation. God loves the entire lump, but it is through the leaven and the salt he is able to perform some of his most mighty acts. Numbers obsess us. We are right to want to see the church grow and go from strength to strength. But numbers are a by-product and, often, a distraction. It is the quality of the church's life which cries out for renewal and revival. And should our prayer be ever answered, members of the church would rejoice in a string of those exciting and lovely characteristics to which I have already referred: love for one another; love for the scriptures; love for the blessed sacrament; love of truth; reverence for the sexuality in every person; love of earth; love for the poor; love of prayer; love of song. These are the gifts of the spirit which I covet for the church – not the dramatic or sensational 'gifts' which have become all the rage, but the 'solid joys and lasting treasure' to which John Newton's hymn refers.

The longing to possess 'miraculous' abilities and to astound others with stunning displays is an insidious temptation frequently associated with those who pray for 'revival'. The psychology behind the desire is not hard to unravel, and has a great deal to do with power, manipulation and self-aggrandisement. It is perilously close to the 'magical Messiah' temptation rejected by Jesus at the outset of his ministry. Of course, beautiful and mysterious things occur wherever God is loved and faithfully served. And in a church which had been touched afresh by the Holy Spirit, more and greater wonders could be expected. There are always occasions for thankfulness and quiet gladness. They are not 'proofs' to wave before an unbelieving world, but holy extras from a tender Giver, and tokens of love.

The church stands in need of a revival of substance, not the ephemeral gloss of a nine days' wonder. We need deep treatment from the Holy Spirit, not superficial titillation. If the quickening power of God was unleashed upon the church in

England, the tiny remnant would swiftly become a potent remnant. England would notice the change. There would be a new feeling in the air.

So much for revival of the church. What of the revival of the nation? The two ideas, though related, are not synonymous. The church's active membership represents only a small segment of the nation's entire population: but England itself needs a revival! Its inner fabric needs renewing; the soul of its people needs cleansing and reinvigorating. Fine words! But do they mean anything? What *would* constitute a revival of the nation? If its rampant materialism could in some way be assuaged, and its people encouraged to look upon the world with greater reverence and upon each other with greater compassion, a new spirit would infuse this land of ours. And that *would* be a revival worth having! Not quite a new heaven and a new earth, maybe, but a promising start.

Try to imagine it! In an England revitalized, there would be a fresh interest in religion. It would manifest itself in the rediscovery of reverence and wonder, and respect for holy things. The aura which surrounds and radiates from ancient sites and old church buildings would be sensed and valued; and those who serve the community by maintaining its religious institutions would be recognized as people playing a positive role in society. At present such attitudes are tottering on the brink of extinction in a generation impoverished by its inability to wonder. Their re-emergence would be a miracle of resurrection.

England revived would vibrate with a new social cohesion, a new sense of justice, a Damascus Road-like realization that every person is precious in the eyes of God. Gone would be the ruthless rivalry of former days; the greed and callous indifference on the one hand, the souring spirit of envy and hatred on the other. Everyone would want to contribute to the common weal, and society would be shaped in a way which encouraged and enabled them to do so. Our brotherly and sisterly love would embrace even those we did not like, the sense of corporate unity being greater than our selfish ambitions and personal prejudices.

No person in this modern world is self-sufficient. Butcher, baker, candlestick maker – we depend manifestly upon the labours of one another. And nobody needs more than three meals a day. Our fundamental requirements are very modest. In our England revived, simple, self-evident truths like these would colour and influence our thinking. Pray God we may come to our senses soon, and begin to act more like the brothers and sisters we are – not in this land alone, but setting the significance of these truisms in an international context! Pray God it does not take a colossal environmental calamity or some unimaginable threat to our planet from hostile external agencies to unite the human race and compel it – at the eleventh hour – to act like a global family! A revived spirit would be one which recognized the treasure, the potential and the miracle of humanity in every person, and responded eagerly and with gladness both in personal attitudes and political choices.

Nobody could consider England revived until a great tide of environmental concern had swept the nation. As I indicated earlier, the present trickle of interest for the well-being of our planet home and all with whom we share it is much to be welcomed; but it must swell to a flood. In a nation renewed children would be taught – in the spirit of St Francis – that all creatures are our relations. A greater knowledge of natural history and a much increased 'feeling' for nature would be evident. The membership of all organizations devoted to various aspects of conservation would increase, while the destruction of important natural habitat, sites of special scientific interest and areas of outstanding natural beauty would cease. Even more significantly, some of the great damage already inflicted would begin to be corrected and made good. Threatened species would be saved. Developments like these would be among the most revealing indicators of the depth and reality of the nation's revival. Reverence for the environment is not merely a 'spiritual' but a profoundly religious attitude. It is good, practical common sense, too! But the fate of the bittern and the natter-jack toad are not academic issues with, at best, a tourist-potential dimension attached. By our attitude to such matters we demonstrate whether or not we possess that sense of 'oneness' with the creation which is possibly the most obviously missing vital ingredient in today's world. Its absence is grievous and threatening, but a nation revived would possess it in abundance.

An England which had rediscovered its soul would find, also, that it possessed a new sense of national identity, a development some would view suspiciously and regard as anachronistic but which I would applaud and welcome. It would not be narrow and nasty. It would be broad, inclusive, modern, generous and welcoming. England revived would be aware of its history, and at ease. Its people would celebrate roots which are wonderfully rich in their diversity. Celts, Romans, Saxons; Danes, Normans, Huguenots; and more recently, men and women from places like Kingston and the Punjab. Today, all these are the English; and a national revival would include the forging of fresh, deep, vital ties of kinship and unity.

I am not only a patriot, I am a romantic! Mine is the England of King Arthur, Alfred the Great, Shakespeare, William Blake, Noel Coward and Churchill! If I didn't love it, I wouldn't care whether it experienced a revival or not. But I care deeply. England is a beautiful and fertile land, with a pleasant and temperate climate. God has used its people and made them a channel through which blessings, rich and diverse, have flowed to other nations. My idea of a national revival is not a return to the mythical days of 'Merrie England' – though I must confess that the images of cricket on the village green and elderly ladies cycling through the morning mist to holy communion cause me personally no embarrassment! Would that more were so doing! My prime concern nowadays would be for their safety. But every token of England – every sign, symbol, embodiment of our national spirit – delights me. Hereward the Wake, Robin Hood, choral evensong, Gilbert and Sullivan, church bells, Stanley Matthews – all are part of the pageant of England, all have contributed to its essence and its ethos.

But this romanticism, however thrilling and meaningful to me, is profoundly meaningless to many people: those enduring the blight of the inner cities, those tormented by unemployment, those suffering racial hatred. These are not remotely interested in ancient history and improbable myths, and who can blame them? Neither are those languishing in featureless suburbs or struggling to survive on grim council estates. For them, other issues take precedence. Yet they all need a cause, an identity, events to celebrate, heroes to praise – all things which constitute a unifying sense of nationhood. If the other parts of the United Kingdom have retained a gut feeling of national identity, there is no reason why the English should not discover one too, and be a stronger, more caring community as a result. The Notting Hill Carnival is a dramatic expression of what 'Englishness' means today. So too are institutions like the National Tramway Museum at Crich, in Derbyshire, where nostalgia, immense voluntary effort, painstaking research and remarkable engineering skills are combined in a manner which always strikes me as indefinably but typically English.

A new interest in religion, a new social cohesion, a tide of environmental concern, a reinvigorated national identity – it's all a dream, of course. But are we no longer permitted to see visions and to dream dreams? For none of these thoughts is wholly far-fetched. At various times in England's history, there have been periods of beneficial religious fervour. Insensitivity and indifference to 'otherness' has appeared only recently. Hopes of a just and compassionate social order burned brightly during and immediately after the last war. The destruction of the environment and our fading love for our country are merely recent developments which (we must hope) could, for the most part, be reversed. So I dream without apology! These are some of the pictures that flicker in my mind when I say 'England needs a revival'. Could it happen?

Channels of Revival

The resurrection of our Saviour is the most dramatic illustration of revival to be found in the scriptures or anywhere else. A dead body, filled with energy and new life: and all the work of God alone! That insight is fundamental to any understanding of revival. Whenever organizations or individuals are reanimated, reinvigorated and filled with a new dynamism and a fresh sense of purpose, the source of that energy is God. We may regret, repent, pray, plan or work with unabated zeal, but 'until the spirit be poured upon us from on high' (to use Isaiah's memorable phrase) our hopes are unlikely to be fulfilled. 'The prayer of a righteous man availeth much'; but God cannot be manipulated, neither can divine action be engineered by human endeavour, however well-intended. Revival is a gift, not a phenomenon which we can conjure up for ourselves, or we would have done so, years ago! Our task is to be faithful and true to the light that is in us, and to watch, be alert, and read the signs of the times.

I make these comments not to encourage inactivity but to check and if necessary correct our perspectives. Of course there are things to be done! And, for men and women of religion, repentance and prayer are high on the list, and are seized upon eagerly by God. In a mystery we can only accept, but never understand, the all-sufficient God welcomes and desires prayer – possibly even *requires* prayer – which he weaves into his loving purposes and uses in his eternal work. Visions of the church revived, and of our nation revived, should constantly form the focus of our prayers and worship. And when we are tempted to cry 'How long, O Lord', we should take courage and heart in the knowledge that God has heard and is at work.

Some people feel that since the church is God's special creation, instrument and channel of his grace, the church must experience revival before the nation can be revived. Here, much depends on definition; and I hope I have indicated already that I would not personally find such a simple and clear-cut formula very helpful. The Spirit is active wherever men and women of goodwill pursue truth and righteousness. To me, therefore, it seems obvious that all those who are involved in education in all its aspects have a crucial role to play in the revival of England. In an age of unbelief and non-participation in organized religion, it is in many respects a role more important than that of the priest. I am not an educationalist, and am reluctant to express other than the most general comments on educational matters. But it is upon the quality and content of the education we provide that our best hopes of a national rebirth rest. Those to whom the word 'revival' is intelligible only in a context of fundamentalism, pentecostalism and larger attendances at religious assemblies will not warm to my insistence on the centrality of education, for by 'education' I mean something diametrically opposite to the indoctrination and brain-washing which appeals to certain schools of religious thought. Those, however, with a vision broad enough to set 'revival' in a meaningful modern context, consistent with intellectual integrity, will recognize that it is linked internally with whatever developments occur in the field of education. 'Revival' – if it is to mean anything today – has to embrace a wide range of inter-linked themes. It is about the recovery of a spirit of reverent inquiry; the encouragement of a sense of awe and wonder; the promotion of civic ideals; the fostering of respect and mutual warmth between different cultures; the rediscovery of Christianity's role in our nation's history, the acknowledgment that mysticism and religious experience are honourable and worthwhile pursuits, the instilling of an affection for the planet, and a sense of kinship with all its people. Revival might well mean *more*; but, to merit the name, it could scarcely embrace less than all these things. And, for the most part, they will not be brought to birth in cold and empty churches (or in warm and crowded revival meetings!) They will be fostered and encouraged to blossom in our schools and through our system of education. If we fail, England's prospects of revival look slim. God has never been confined within a 'religious' strait-jacket. The world is his and he is busy within it, happily at ease within 'secular' institutions and ready to employ the services of all men and women of goodwill. Those whose lives are dedicated to the cause of education have assumed a role second to none in its centrality to God's mission and strategy. The hopes of those who long for revival are, in many vital respects, in the hands of our teachers and educationalists.

Christianity has enjoyed a privileged role in our educational system over the years. This is entirely understandable, and in no way discreditable. Christianity has been not only the traditional and established religion of the land; it has itself played a pioneering role in education. It was not present in schools under sufferance; often, it was present because it had *built* the schools! It had built them not only to teach religion, though religion was at the heart of the curriculum. The church built schools because it recognized that education represented one brilliant facet of the light of the gospel. Christ's message of truth and love challenged the darkness not only of sin but of ignorance. Sound learning and careful scholarship were ever expressions of Christianity at its best.

But times have changed. Christianity's privileged position at the heart of England's educational system could not prevent the erosion of belief and the secularization of modern society. Furthermore, the post-war years have seen the emergence of a multi-faith nation in which all the great religions of the world rub shoulders together, and ethnic minorities guard jealously the right to maintain their distinctive customs and traditions. These changing circumstances have created many anomalies within our schools. The content of the religious education curriculum and the inability of many schools to comply with the law on collective daily worship are two areas of continuing important debate. An increasing number of staff are exercising their right neither to lead nor participate in the prescribed worship, and many teachers consider that schools cannot be expected to accept responsibility for promoting daily religious observance when parents themselves do not practise it.

It is plainly not the business of schools to seek to make converts on behalf of the church. At the same time, a majority of the population – even now – would probably feel some regret or unease if all opportunities to explore and express simple forms of worship – and still usually in England Christian worship – were expunged from the school curriculum. I don't know how to proceed. Even when I was a child – which wasn't yesterday – school assemblies did little to quicken the interest of my school-fellows or myself in the Christian faith. Modern assemblies I know are frequently much more imaginative, and I'm anxious that nothing good be thrown away. We cannot afford to do so. It is much to be hoped that before the requirement of a daily act of worship passes into oblivion, a consensus is reached on its replacement. Christians involved in education bear an enormous responsibility. The revival of our country's soul depends heavily upon their decisions and their labours, and members of the church should be aware of the fact more keenly and more prayerfully.

In a recent powerful plea for more specialist teachers of religion, more time in the curriculum and more money for books and equipment, the former Archbishop of York called for avoidance of over-zealous dogmatism and the suggestion that all religions were the same.

Speaking at an education conference in London, which was reported in *The Guardian* of 9 March 1995, Dr Hapgood said:

> We are in danger of producing a morally bewildered generation, and while there is no educationally valid way back to a heavy-handed moralism, there is a responsibility on the education world to help in building some moral foundations . . .
>
> Religious impulses do not disappear when a particular culture finds it hard to handle them. They reappear in other guises, usually ones which have very slender connections with reality as ordinarily perceived.

It would be foolish to over-emphasize the importance of

New Age religion, but the fact that most major bookshops carry shelves of books on astrology and the occult, and various kinds of healing, and keys to self-knowledge, offset by a small row of presentation Bibles and white-bound Books of Common Prayer in a dingy corner, is surely a straw in the wind . . . We have to take seriously the fact there is a lot of religion around in today's world and that the antidote to irrationalism is not irreligion but rational religion . . .

To be religiously literate is nowadays an essential part of growing up to be a responsible, informed citizen.

Dr Hapgood suggested that 'rational' or 'critical' religion was important for schools in its own right. It did justice to the distinctiveness of faith while at the same time encouraging the search for religious reality in terms of questions rather than answers.

I cannot help feeling that my 'three circles' approach to religion is relevant to the teaching of religion in England today, and harmonizes with the words of the Archbishop. It treats the subject in a non-authoritarian and rational manner, initially by identifying the three core constituents of religion: awe and mystery; ethics and morality; doctrine and worship. Is it fanciful to detect a reflection of the doctrine of the Trinity in these inter-related ingredients? The first section opens the subject in a way intended deliberately to include everybody, and under an umbrella wide enough to embrace themes of an endless and fascinating variety. Reverence for life; the un-fathomable mysteries of time and space; bio-diversity and interdependence; the beauty of nature; the appeal of music; the mystery of self-awareness; mystical experience as a widespread and non-dogmatic fact of life (by mountains, rivers, sea-shores, as well as in old buildings and religious assemblies); in fact, any theme likely to engender attitudes of curiosity and wonder and gentleness. For these, rather than doses of raw biblical teaching – or any other sectarian inculcation – are the spawning grounds and birth-place of the genuinely religious spirit.

The second section confronts the inescapable question of how we deal with the mystery of other centres of self-consciousness, i.e. other people! Again, the range of topics covering personal and social relationships is wide and inviting – everything from international affairs and Third World development to sexual ethics, political service, personal responsibility, kindness to neighbours and loyalty to friends. How should we treat one another? That is the question each human being has to address. (And, for Christians, with their faith in a God who was incarnate, it is perhaps the ultimate question.) 'Where shall we look for advice, suggestions, insights? There has been no shortage of great thinkers, philosophers and religious teachers down the centuries. Their conclusions are worth studying. Among them all, the teaching of Jesus has historically played a prominent part in shaping our national character and – purely in moral and ethical terms – is still well-worth examining . . .' It is in such logical yet tentative and deferential terms that the person of Jesus should be introduced. But long before this point is reached, much territory can be explored, of a rich and creative nature, and in a manner which need not cause embarrassment, resentment or offence, even in a multi-cultural society. The awakening of interest; the kindling of an awareness that there *is* a journey of discovery to be made into a world of values and – in the broadest sense – spiritual experience: these are the tasks of the dedicated teacher.

The third section of my approach to religion is clearly the most sensitive in an educational context, but the study of elementary church history, the great stories of the Bible, and the doctrines of the Christian church can all be undertaken with a simple objectivity which neither embarrasses nor affronts the intellectual integrity of the student. It is the move from there to specific acts of worship which is the tricky part, and where I retreat – not from cowardice, but with humility – to leave those with experience and expertise to lead our thinking. To attempt to foist the practice of Christianity on to a captive young audience is distasteful; yet a refusal to share something meaningful and beautiful (simply because we, personally, have abandoned it) would constitute wilful neglect. Nothing is more important than the education of our children. There will be no revival in England of anything worthwhile if we do not teach each new generation the wideness and the wonder of religion.

Those who have reached mature years have become shaped by their experiences and set in their ways. It is the children who are our treasure and our great hope. Modern families come in all shapes and sizes, but everything which promotes loving family relationships and emphasizes the importance of the home should be encouraged. And we all meet children and young people, even those of us who are not teachers. It is important that we learn to take them seriously and treat them with respect, firmness, fairness and tolerance. By so doing, we may be making our own small contribution towards the fashioning of a new and more enlightened generation.

Any revival of our national life will involve political decisions, and at first glance, our need of renewal seems to provide a perfect illustration of the-chicken-or-the-egg conundrum. Society will not be renewed until enlightened men pursue enlightened policies; but until society produces enlightened men, enlightened policies will not be produced! Providentially, the dilemma is never quite so stark! Even in the darkest days, there are always men and women of vision trying to make their voices heard. If we long to see something of the old England reborn in modern guise, it is to them we must listen.

Something vital has died in England, leaving it a different and poorer place. This, again, is not the forum for a detailed political analysis, nor am I the person to provide it. But these words of MP Tony Wright, in a *Guardian* article of 29 May 1995, struck a vibrant chord. They have clear relevance to the theme of revival and its connection to political activity, and for present purposes, they must suffice.

The resonance of the language of community and citizenship speaks to what has been lost. The privatization and fragmentation of social life now has to be matched by the energetic renewal of public institutions, spaces and cultures.

But this cannot be in the old way or on the old terms. It demands endless ingenuity and imagination. The erosion of community produced by social exclusion and joblessness requires more than the pressing of a few macro-economic levers. The renewal of public services does not mean a return to old models of organization and delivery but the development of new ones. Welfare to be reshaped to fit a changed society. Public and private provision will connect in a whole variety of previously unexpected ways.

None of this is easy or straightforward; much of it is difficult and daunting. It will require great political intelligence and discipline . . .

There is nothing more frustrating for a writer than to recognize the importance of a particular subject, yet personally to possess first-hand knowledge so slight as to be negligible! I have dared already to refer to the importance of religious education, without having myself any experience as an educationalist. Now, with a brevity all will applaud, I want to enter a plea which will surprise many: a plea for the retention of some form of establishment.

Those who want to see a revival of religion in England should think long and hard before adding their voices to those clamouring for the disestablishment of the Church of England. It is a luxury we cannot afford, a piece of territory which, in our present condition, it would be madness voluntarily to surrender. After many years of worker-priest ministry, my reluctant impression is that the Free Churches cut no ice in England today. Among non-churchgoers, their existence goes unnoticed. In my part of the country, Roman Catholics fare little better. The fact that the Pope is a prominent international figure gives them a slightly higher rating in the national consciousness, but the papal stance on sexual matters has turned this increased awareness into a liability, and filled the minds of many honest men and women with cold contempt. Only the Church of England retains (by its finger tips) a residual hold on the minds of English non-worshippers – for good or ill! It does so, not because its people are more faithful or its prayers are more efficacious. It does so because it is the established church.

I have repeatedly expressed my strong belief that the Church of England has failed the nation in this second half of the twentieth century by not recognizing its moment of destiny, and by scuppering the Anglican-Methodist conversations which could have transformed England. But there are times when I almost feel sorry for it. When Methodist chapels close – and where Roman Catholics have never penetrated – the church-by-law-established juggles and struggles to maintain some skeletal form of presence and ministry. No part of the kingdom is left uncovered. Even today, that counts for something.

When society requires a solemn ceremony to express a religious sentiment or noble aspiration, it is the bishop or his local representative to whom the opportunity falls. Without strong links between church and state, many such opportunities (one suspects) would not be shared more widely, but would simply vanish. I see the coronation service as the outstanding illustration of the strategic and religious benefits of establishment. Many will mock and dismiss my view as romanticism run riot, but the conviction remains that the soul of England – its indefinable essence, its sense of nationhood – has its roots in the coronation service. Establishment opens many doors from the lowest to the highest levels of society, providing opportunities of meeting and influencing which are too precious to jettison casually.

There are, of course, obvious pitfalls; and there is a price to be paid. And more than one form of relationship between church and state is possible. Today, the disunity of the English church weakens the impact of establishment, as both the burdens and the opportunities fall entirely upon the Anglicans. If the contract between church and state in England could have been with a united church, the potential would have been even greater. (I had hoped to spend my ministry in a rapidly uniting church, helping to develop a broader form of establishment.) However, we must begin with an acceptance of where we are today. The nature of establishment may alter, but its surrender would diminish the nation. The choice, as so often in politics, church affairs and life itself, is between a notional purity (accompanied by a diminished influence bordering on the impotent) and a willingness to participate, compromise, get involved and get dirty (but with a fair chance of being able to contribute and achieve *something*). I have never had any trouble deciding which approach harmonizes more closely with the principle which lay behind Christ's incarnation.

Here endeth the simplistic and confused thoughts of a Free Churchman on establishment! I have espoused the risk of ridicule gladly, however, because I sense we could be drifting towards disestablishment almost by default. Unlike some, I believe that such a development would only postpone the day when the breath of new life was breathed among the people of England, and the church touched by a true spirit of revival.

As for the English church, in *all* its branches: how ought it to wait and prepare for the gift of revival to be given? The church allows that it possesses treasure in earthen vessels – something beyond price by which the people of England would be immeasurably enriched, could they but have the scales removed from their eyes, and be made to see. But how to impart this priceless pearl? How to make its existence known? How to serve the present age faithfully, intelligibly, effectively? The church needs a booster dose of what happened on that first Whit Sunday. But, meanwhile . . . ? Again, I shall disappoint. I am not heading towards a neat finale, with a detailed summary and a programme of action for the church in England which will guarantee a swift and dramatic divine response. As a matter of fact, my confidence in the church has taken some nasty knocks. There are days when I seriously wonder if it's up to the job.

As the church waits longingly and hopefully for a revival of its life, and for a quickening of the nation, and for thousands to discover for themselves the fulfilment and satisfaction to be experienced in a life of Christian discipleship, there are, of course, many areas in which it should be particularly alert, open and prepared. Chief among these are unity, worship and mission. The first is rather like shutting the stable door after the horse has bolted. Having fluffed the best opportunity many of us are likely ever to see to make telling progress on this critical front, we reaped a bitter harvest as a consequence. Now it is imperative that English Christians ignore denominational boundaries at every opportunity, and hope that God will forgive us, help us to learn from one another and make us start behaving like the community of love we are supposed to be.

A similar foreboding surrounds the question of our worship. Perhaps I alone feel like this! But for me dignity has gone, together with reverence, mystery and that vital sense of 'otherness'. Without these, it is hard to sustain a serious attitude to religion of any kind; this is the failure which may yet prove our undoing. Men and women need to worship, and we should be professional enough not only to provide forms which are reasonably meaningful but also convey the serene impression that it is a perfectly normal human activity. Increasingly, this relaxed modern approach to public worship is allied with the insidious fundamentalist/pentecostalist infection, and produces bright simple assertions – usually from scripture – at every opportunity. This combination is lethal. If, having dispensed with the numinous, we insist on confronting the people of England with a series of outrageous intellectual propositions, couched in language which conveys no meaning, we should not be surprised if they look the other way. Phrases with meanings profound and precious to those of us who share the faith – phrases like 'Christ died for your sins' – are simply incomprehensible to those without faith, and are met with utter blankness and total indifference.

Forget the crowded gospel halls. Numbers are a by-product and distraction. The fact to remember is that an overwhelming majority of the English are fast becoming immune to Christian or indeed any other kind of religious slogans. One of our best hopes of piercing their materialism and their indifference is by endeavouring to provide or create the conditions in which it becomes possible for them to receive a religious experience, on the rare occasions when circumstances demand a religious rite. That is why the quality of our worship is so important. It is our front line of mission.

As for mission itself, it has become extraordinarily difficult to think of anything new to say! so much has been written and spoken and so many brave ventures implemented – yet still the spark is not fanned to a flame! Perhaps we continue to look for the wrong kind of success – the numbers game, again. No work attempted for God is not honoured and used by God, even when we are not permitted to see the end result. But this must not be used as an excuse! All Christian people should recognize the missionary obligation inherent in their faith, and endeavour to maintain a humble but buoyant witness before the world. Samuel Chadwick's pithy old slogan, 'Evangelize or perish', captures a fundamental truth in a haunting and memorable manner. And were I *really* to tell the truth, I would need to admit that despite the brave words and valiant efforts of many Christian people to penetrate areas of society beyond the church – to witness and to provide a Christian presence – I do not feel that enough of us do all that we could. Church-based duties absorb much time and energy. Without these the church would, indeed, be in a bad way! But nurture those contacts and commitments outside the church too, however lowly and insignificant they appear. The link you are providing, without necessarily ever uttering an overtly religious sentiment, could provide the Spirit of God with a channel of opportunity, and a vehicle for his grace.

My personal difficulty, however, will have become evident to the discerning! As the church waits and prays for revival – the revival of the nation and the revival of its own life – the three areas I have identified as meriting particular faithfulness are areas in which I fear that the church has either conspicuously failed (unity), got it wrong (worship) or could have done better (mission). Many may find it hard to forgive what they will view as arrogant pessimism – but I hope they will try. Those inner convictions are hard enough to live with, without attracting the obloquy of faithful men and women whose labours I admire so much. I hope I am not arrogant. I am trying to be prophetic. And, ultimately, I am not pessimistic. My assessments are admittedly sobering. But I am thrown back, continually, on the living God. And I wait eagerly, with wonder and with baited breath, to see what he will do next.

The church is his bride, his special creation, his chosen instrument, the object of his most tender love. But he does not work through it in a manner which is exclusively collective. He works through me, and through you. Could the revival begin in us?

11

Revive Us! Revive Me!

One night, at the time that I was writing this little book, I had a dream unlike any other I had ever experienced. It remained vivid in my mind when I awoke and never faded completely. In my dream, I was engaged upon this very work, and was busy typing the last page. I brought it to an impressive climax with a quotation from those well-known verses of Ross Parker and Hugh Charles:

> There'll always be an England,
>   And England shall be free –
> If England means as much to you
>   As England means to me.

At first, still half-awake, I was excited at the thought that my final rallying-call had been dictated in a dream! In the harsh light of day, I reconsidered. The story, however, seemed too good to ignore completely and, in any case, the more I pondered the more I realized that the quotation *could* be interpreted in an interesting and valuable way. The Christian gospel is indeed about freedom. Jesus promised: 'Ye shall know the truth, and the truth shall make you free.' An overwhelming experience of liberation awaits the men and women of England when they recognize the truth embodied uniquely in Jesus. The centrality of love to human life; the harmony of love with the flow of the universe; the demonstration, the promise, and the victory of love, seen in the cross and the Easter garden. This is the knowledge which brings true freedom and liberty of the spirit, which need never be surrendered; which imparts a quiet joy, burning within us, and a peace which passeth all understanding. 'If the Son therefore shall make you free, you shall be free indeed.'

This precious freedom of spirit is not an attitude of arrogance and superiority. Rather, it is the calm confidence which stems from an allegiance to another Kingdom, an unseen realm, where different values hold sway. It is the secret strength which flows from being anchored and grounded in love. It is the composed, unshakeable awareness that 'All shall be well.'

England would be holy and happy if thousands more of her people enjoyed this liberty. It has little to do with the assertion of rights, but everything to do with release from selfishness and being therefore more completely at the service of the community. Oh, that England might be free! – that every power that darkens or diminishes our national life should be banished, and our country distinguished by that righteousness which exalteth a nation!

That hour is not yet. England remains in thrall to the trivial, the materialistic, the ungenerous, and the base. The church knows how these shackles can be snapped and the nation released and revived. Yet the church, as an institution, has boxed itself into a corner, its influence ever-diminishing as a result of its unfaithfulness and a series of self-inflicted wounds. Our hopes for the future rest now upon the faithfulness of its individual members, upon people like you and me. Each of us is an expression of the church. We may not pass resolutions or harry governments or make public pronouncements or get on the telly. But that isn't the way God works! Put simply, the crucial question is this. Are you willing for the religious revival England needs to begin in you? This is the heart of the matter. Each of us must be prepared for God to work in us, personally, whatever he longs to effect in the nation at large. Never mind the institution in its holy cumbersomeness! God loves it, and will continue to protect and use it; and we all belong beneath its great umbrella. But the seeds of hope and renewal lie with those whose hearts are open to the living God, and hunger and thirst for a revival of their own inner life and spiritual vision. And here is the second link with my dream: the crucial element of personal responsibility. God is in charge; the work is his. But within the embrace of his almighty providence and his steadfast and loving purposes, 'England free' depends on you and me. The spirit may take the nation by storm, rushing through all the institutions of church and state, overwhelming those who doubt with incontrovertible signs and wonders and turning the hearts of the disobedient to the wisdom of the just. Let it be so! But, while we wait, let our own hearts and lives stand ever ajar to the sweet, transforming influence of our reviving God! Revive us, O Lord. Revive me.

England needs above all men and women who have seen the beauty of Jesus and whose imagination has been gripped by the vision. This experience transcends questions of intellectual assent or specific dogmas. In any case, the distinctions between reason and faith are usually blurred. Faith can burn brightly or it can dim to the point of extinction. But a true glimpse of Jesus, and of the world as he envisaged it, has a powerfully persistent quality which, once seen, is never forgotten. This experience lies at the heart of Christian discipleship, producing mystical experiences for some and political incentives for others. (It should produce both!) The vision has a powerful, self-authenticating quality which appeals equally to the heart, the mind and the imagination.

Those who have been touched by the nobility of Christ's teaching, with its emphasis upon neighbourliness, community and care of the weak and vulnerable, should cling to the picture, pursue the prize and not be ashamed to attribute its source. By so doing they contribute to England's revival, even when they possess no church allegiance whatsoever. Personally, I often wish such people could find it in themselves to *pretend* to believe! I suppose 'pretend' is the wrong word, for religion is about nothing if it is not the truth. But the dream or the vision, rather than absolute doctrinal convictions, is the more important. Some profess the latter, yet betray no evidence of having been captured by the former. And even a minimal participation in the church's liturgy – hearing the word occasionally or receiving the blessed sacrament – helps to nourish the vision and keep it alive.

Those upon whom Christ's words have had a more dynamic

and personal impact – and who are to be found still within the fellowship of the church – are privileged and highly favoured. To them has fallen a great opportunity and a solemn responsibility. At his perpetual disposal, God requires people to be open constantly to the promptings of his Spirit, eager to make new discoveries, anxious to grow in the things of God and willing to be agents of revival. This means being filled with new life themselves: then being filled again and again! Those who have experienced shame, then a sense of forgiveness, then a long string of spiritual sensations – joy and peace and inner strength and rare moments of wonder and glory – can never forget those events without denying everything best within them. Even when the church drives them to distraction and despair, they cannot turn their back on Jesus.

In faith, and with no clear idea of God's overall strategy, they can but be true to the light that is in them. God asks no more: and he is able to use their humble, dedicated service in his reviving, renewing, healing and reinvigorating work. Let us not hide behind excuses like 'the state of the church'. Only God can sort that out! In the meantime there is work to be done – and God will honour your efforts. Though like Elijah we imagine (wrongly) that we are labouring alone, those labours are contributing under God's providence to the revival of the church and the nation, and to the ultimate victory of love. We must dare to believe it!

Speaking a word of testimony is a good, old-fashioned nonconformist custom. My personal experience over the forty years since my teenage conversion offers confirmation that even the simple religious experience of a child can last a lifetime, and that a vigorous personal witness – in pursuit of the vision – remains possible, even when the church has broken your heart. My school friends and my workmates were the first objects of my missionary zeal. Both groups resisted, firmly though not unkindly. It was the mid 1950s, and I had divined immediately – almost intuitively – that the church in England was in trouble. I was encouraged to offer for the ministry and the Methodist Church wrapped a dog-collar around my neck (on Sundays, at least) when I was still only nineteen. My attitude to the church has never changed. From the outset it was a mixture of tender, filial affection mingled with an exasperation and – on occasion – a loathing shocking in its intensity. *But the vision would never go away.* 'The old, old story of Jesus and his love' has never lost its place in my imagination. Alarmed at what I perceived as the church's growing isolation from the main stream of the nation's life, I insisted on implementing a worker-priest pattern of ministry. My desolation at the foundering of the Anglican-Methodist unity scheme reinforced my determination to persist in my new ministry, and I have continued in the same city, earning my living as a bus driver, for the best part of thirty years (which have passed with astonishing swiftness). From my cab I have watched as a long stream of clergy have come and gone. As they have moved to new responsibilities, my own roots have only grown deeper in the life of the community, frequently providing help and occasionally causing offence with the gospel of Christ. Throughout this period God has provided a string of opportunities of which I could never have dreamed. In addition to my basic twin roles of Methodist minister and bus driver, I have also been shop steward, sheriff, company director and newspaper columnist, and with a few other hats worn from time to time, too. If I don't seem to have converted anyone, the strange thing is that it doesn't seem to matter! Despite all reservations about the church, God has permitted me to pursue a vigorous personal ministry which, looking back, I would like to think has been a positive rather than neutral or negative influence within the community, preparing the way of the Lord by keeping alive the embers upon which our reviving God must blow.

Cardinal Danneels, Archbishop of Mechlin-Brussels said recently: 'People do not want a strict, authoritarian line. They want a pastor. They want a bridge back to the church that is deep in them, a church they are away from. I have tried to be a bridge.'

Cardinals or bus drivers, men and women at the heart of the ecclesiastical system or perched precariously on the edge – it doesn't matter to God. Those who are prepared to *be* revived, God will use *to* revive. Ultimately, it will not rest with synods, parliaments or church assemblies. It is upon *us* God is relying. 'Ye must be born again' insisted Jesus to the wise but bewildered Nicodemus. A new dream, a new vision, a new principle must be grafted into human hearts! Thinking about the life of Jesus of Nazareth, letting the beauty of his teaching reach deep into our hearts and minds and murmuring 'yes' in a glad response, never to be revoked – this is where revival begins. And having begun there, in such flinty and unpromising soil, it could break out again, anywhere!

> Spirit of the living God, fall afresh on me!
> Break me, melt me, mould me, fill me!
> Spirit of the living God, fall afresh on me!

England needs a revival, not just an intellectual rebirth or renaissance, but a revival of religion. And not merely religion in any shape or form, worthy and welcome as the great religions are (and many of the New Age insights too), but a rediscovery of its historic Christian faith which is entwined inextricably with its sense of nationhood and its collective sub-conscious. Let other nations choose! But we chose Christ, and that choice shaped our nation and made it the attractive phenomenon it remains. Now is the time to be true to our own selves. England without a strong Christian awareness is not a nation come of age, but a nation diminished.

It is a curious fact that precious insights, and near-inexpressible truths, are sometimes best captured incidentally, or conveyed most memorably in comic or trivial events. For me, for example, the best of the *Dad's Army* television series touched a chord – on occasion ridiculously moving – which said something vital about England. Conversely, while straining to keep a sense of proportion, I cannot help seeing tell-tale signs of England's decline in incidents which in themselves are minor and inconsequential, yet which seem to carry within them seeds which promise a bitter harvest. Litter, from takeaways consumed in the churchyard in the small hours, simply dropped to the ground with a waste-bin just yards away; and this

accompanied by the beheading of the flowering tulips . . .
Incidents come no more trivial than that! Nobody hurt, no
serious harm done. Simply beer and high spirits! I know and I
agree. But a heaviness lingers in my heart, too, and it will not go
away. It isn't the bank robberies and other *causes célèbres* which
throw me. They have always occurred, the criminal actions of
an anti-social minority. It is the daily evidence, the chain of
unloveliness and unkindness, witnessed in actions and attitudes
not necessarily unlawful, which gives the game away. An
ugliness has crept into our hearts, a vulgarity, a lack of
courtesy. There is scant knowledge of God, love for our
neighbour or sense of community. We are not handling
competently the rapid changes being thrust upon us by the
advance of science. Political changes have left many feeling
disillusioned, resentful and rejected, and the poor, the young
and the old have had to bear the brunt. Tossed first one way and
then another, millions seem rudderless on a sea of uncertainty.
What an opportunity for those in whose lives revival has
become a reality to reaffirm their commitment and redouble
their efforts! What a moment to busy themselves in those works
and spheres through which the Spirit of God might choose to
release a revival of religion throughout the land! If not Ross
Parker and Hugh Charles then Blake, surely, for the grand
finale?

> I will not cease from mental fight,
>   Nor shall my sword sleep in my hand,
> Till we have built Jerusalem
>   In England's green and pleasant land.

I would end there, gladly, unapologetically and without scruple.
Jerusalem causes me no problems! I notice it doesn't appear in
the latest hymn book of my denomination, but that doesn't
surprise me. I know only that, over the years, I have conducted
the singing of it in my local pub times without number – lusty,
full-blooded renderings, containing more genuine passion than
many a modern service. I suppose the people who compile
hymnals are not asked very often to minister in public houses –

another example, perhaps, of an apparently trivial matter revealing an important and in this instance salutary truth.

Blake's visionary lines fail as a summary of my thoughts on England's need of revival only because their emphasis is upon our *own* efforts and obligations. Such commitment is indeed the only possible response in those who have caught a glimpse – of whatever kind – fleeting, mystical or intellectual – of the holy lamb of God and the countenance divine. There will be no revival, of the church, of England, of the world, if those who claim to have seen the King in all his glory do nothing about it.

Ultimately, however, revival is not *our* work. We can sing and pray, study and strive. We can do everything to ensure our own part is done faithfully. But revival is a gift, not a work. If the gift is withheld, perhaps it is withheld for a reason. We must wait, as we wait each advent: eagerly, anxiously, expectantly; and as we wait, pray with St John the Divine:

Even so, come, Lord Jesus.